ALASKA'S HISTORY

T0001641

Tlingit girl with ancient totems. Winter and Pond photo, about 1895.

ALASKA'S HISTORY

*The People, Land, and Events
of the North Country*

REVISED EDITION

HARRY RITTER

ALASKA
NORTHWEST
BOOKS®

Revised Edition first printed in 2020

Library of Congress Cataloging-in-Publication Data

Names: Ritter, Harry, author.
Title: Alaska's history : the people, land, and events of the North Country /
    Harry Ritter.Other titles: People, land, and events of the North Country
Description: Revised edition. | [Berkeley, California] : West Margin Press,
    [2020] | Series: WestWinds Press pocket guide | Includes bibliographical
    references and index. | Summary: "A travel-sized history book on
    Alaska, with up-to-date information and historical photographs about
    the Last Frontier's past and present"—Provided by publisher.
Identifiers: LCCN 2019026002 (print) | LCCN 2019026003 (ebook) |
    ISBN 9781513262727 (paperback) | ISBN 9781513262734 (hardback) |
    ISBN 9781513262741 (ebook)
Subjects: LCSH: Alaska—History.
Classification: LCC F904 .R58 2020 (print) | LCC F904 (ebook) |
    DDC 979.8—dc23
LC record available at https://lccn.loc.gov/2019026002
LC ebook record available at https://lccn.loc.gov/2019026003

Cartographer: Vikki Leib
Indexer: Sheila Ryan
Cover: 'The Trickster,' David Boxley, Tsimshian, 1988. Private collection.

Proudly distributed by Ingram Publisher Services.

Published by Alaska Northwest Books®, an imprint of West Margin Press

WEST
MARGIN
PRESS

WestMarginPress.com

WEST MARGIN PRESS
Publishing Director: Jennifer Newens
Marketing Manager: Angela Zbornik
Editor: Olivia Ngai
Design & Production: Rachel Lopez Metzger
Desgin Intern: Michelle Montano

CONTENTS

Residents of Skagway, 1898, including Soapy Smith (fourth from the right).

EXPLORERS, ADVENTURERS, AND NATURALISTS: AMERICA'S NEW FRONTIER

ALASKA IN THE TWENTIETH CENTURY: FROM TERRITORY TO STATEHOOD

GEOGRAPHY, CLIMATE, AND NATURAL EXTREMES

Mount Katmai on the Alaska Peninsula,
one year after its great eruption of June 6, 1912 (see p.96)

ACKNOWLEDGMENTS

Among the people who have nurtured my interest in Alaska's history, sometimes unknowingly, I wish to thank in particular Darrel Amundsen, Monty Elliot, Gary Ferngren, and Sue Hackett, as well as Ron Valentine, Director of Operations of World Explorer Cruises. I am especially indebted to Marlene Blessing and Ellen Wheat of Alaska Northwest Books for supporting the idea of a popular history of Alaska, and to Betty Watson for designing the book. In the later stages of writing, Nolan Hester provided invaluable editorial suggestions which resulted in a much-improved manuscript. Ted C. Hinckley, Catherine and Bill Ouweneel, and Roy Potter kindly agreed to read the manuscript in its late form. I also wish to thank Richard Engeman and the staff of the Special Collections Division of the University of Washington Libraries, India M. Spartz of the Alaska Historical Library, Marge Heath of Rasmuson Library at the University of Alaska/ Fairbanks, Toni Nagel of the Whatcom Museum of History and Art, Ken Southerland of Sealaska Corporation, Sara Timby and Linda Long of the Special Collections of Stanford University Libraries, Mike Connors of the Port of Bellingham, Fred Goodman of Bellingham, Doug Charles of the Totem Heritage Center in Ketchikan, and several colleagues at Western Washington University: Janet Collins, Gene Hoerauf, Ed Vajda, Ray McInnis, Virginia Beck of Wilson Library's Special Collections, and especially Jim Scott, Director of Western's Center for Pacific Northwest Studies.

For the book's second edition, I want to thank Jennifer Newens and the West Margin Press team for inviting me to undertake the revision. Very special thanks, as well, to Tricia Brown and Leza Madsen for their helpful suggestions.

Thanks, above all, to my wife, Marian, and son, Alan, without whose inspiration and support this book would not have been written.

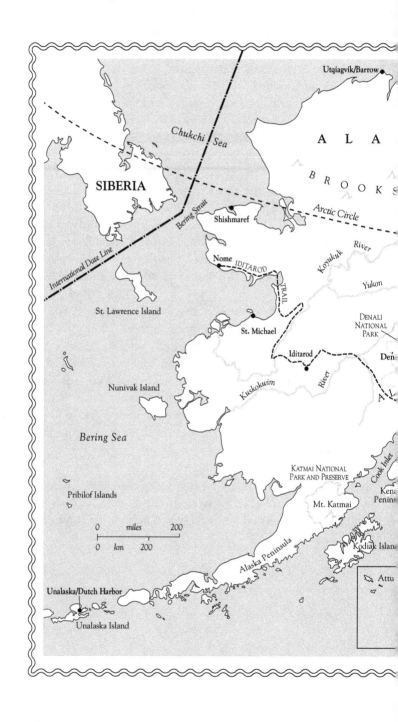

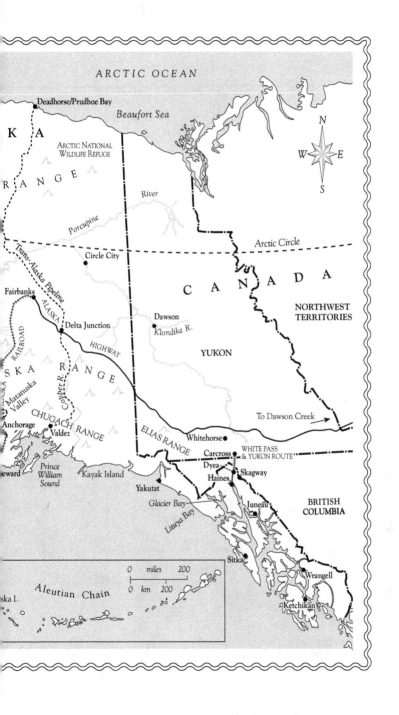

ARCTIC OCEAN

Deadhorse/Prudhoe Bay

Beaufort Sea

K A

ARCTIC NATIONAL
WILDLIFE REFUGE

R A N G E

River

Porcupine

N

W   E

S

Trans-Alaska Pipeline

Arctic Circle

Circle City

C A N A D A

Fairbanks

NORTHWEST
TERRITORIES

ALASKA

Delta Junction

Dawson

RAILROAD

Klondike R.

HIGHWAY

YUKON

S K A   R A N G E

Matanuska
Valley

Copper R.

CHUGACH RANGE

To Dawson Creek

Anchorage

Valdez

ELIAS RANGE

Whitehorse

Carcross

WHITE PASS
& YUKON ROUTE

ska I.

*Prince
William
Sound*

Kayak Island

Dyea

Skagway

eward

Haines

Yakutat

BRITISH
COLUMBIA

Glacier Bay

Juneau

Lituya Bay

Sitka

Aleutian Chain

0   *miles*   200

0   km   200

Wrangell

Ketchikan

Snug Corner Cove, Prince William Sound. Drawing by John Webber, 1778.

ALASKA:
THE GREAT LAND

Alaska, Past and Present

Gold and silver doors, St. Michael's Cathedral, Sitka, late 1800s.

Alaska's human history—from the prehistoric arrival of the earliest Siberian hunters to today's Arctic Slope oil exploration—is unified by one simple but grand theme: people's efforts to wrest a living from the region's vast natural riches despite its extreme conditions.

Nature endowed the Great Land with wealth, scenery, and a scope surpassed by few regions of the earth. Alaska is a virtual subcontinent: Twice the size of Texas, it contains 16 percent of the United States' land area. But its population remains small. At the time of the U.S. purchase in 1867, Alaska had about 30,000 people, more than 29,000 of them Native American. By 2018, despite statehood and the oil boom, its population had grown to an estimated 738,000.

Over the past 275 years, Alaska has seen a series of boom-and-bust "rushes" to exploit the land: rushes for fur, gold, copper, salmon, and oil. Some people came and stayed, simply because Alaska is like nowhere else—wild, extreme, and amazing. Still, the aim often has been to take the rewards of the land and sea, then enjoy them somewhere else. Many Alaskans see a recurring theme of neglect by federal authorities and exploitation by "outside interests." While the notion is easily exaggerated, the fact remains that today, decades after becoming a state, much of Alaska's economic fate remains under control of the Lower 48. Much of the Alaska fishing fleet, for example, is based not in Alaska, but in Washington state.

Over the past six decades, the development of a modern tourism industry has brought millions of visitors to the once-remote frontier in a veritable "tourist rush." The more daring travelers motor north via the Alaska Highway, built during World War II. But most come by air or sea. The state-owned ferry system, the "Alaska Marine Highway," has linked southeastern Alaska to British Columbia and Washington state since the 1960s. Each year, thousands of ferry travelers experience the stunning sea and landscapes of the Inside Passage. In the 1970s, the cruise ship industry met that same growing tourist demand by offering summertime excursions to the icy spectacles of Glacier Bay National Park and the Gulf of Alaska.

Visitors are drawn to Alaska by the region's wild beauty and storied past. Alaska's history has not always been happy. For traditional Native cultures as well as for some animal species, it is no exaggeration to say that at times it has been catastrophic. Yet to ignore the past denies us the chance to learn for the future. This book aims to supply a concise, informative, and entertaining account of Alaska's history: at times heroic and surprising, foolish and sad, but always colorful and often downright thrilling.

Aleut baskets. Photo by Edward Curtis, 1899.

NATIVE TRADITIONS

ALASKA'S FIRST PEOPLES

Eskimo village, Plover Bay (Siberia). Photo by Edward Curtis, 1899.

Alaska's original discoverers, most authorities believe, were pre-historic hunters from Siberia. In a series of periodic migrations they followed game onto a now-vanished Bering Sea land bridge that—depending on changing sea levels—sometimes connected Asia and North America to create an ancient landmass known as "Beringia." The timing and details of these events are matters of robust debate and conjecture, fueled by ongoing climate research, language studies, archaeological discoveries, and DNA analysis.

Around 14–12,000 years ago the last ice age ended, sea levels rose, and the land bridge was permanently submerged. Alaska and Siberia were severed by the Bering Strait, 56 miles wide. As rising temperatures opened ice-free corridors in the continental interior, some hunters moved south to become ancestors of today's lower North and South American Indians. Even earlier, recent excavations suggest, some migrants may have traveled in boats along the coast, as glaciers receded into fjords. Some later waves of land-bridge migrants stayed north, however, to become ancestors of today's distinctive, broadly-defined Alaska Native cultures: Indian, Unangâx/Aleut, Eskimo, and Alutiiq/Sugpiaq.

Each of these groups created its own rich spirit world and unique ways of surviving, and even prospering, in the often-harsh North. For hunters, aided by snowshoes, dogsleds, and a deep knowledge of weather patterns, the frozen landscape was a highway rather than a frightening barrier. Likewise, for coastal kayakers and canoeists, the cold ocean straits and passages became trade and communication arteries. And despite the northern latitude, the land could be generous, especially along the coasts where fish, waterfowl, and marine mammals made leisure, and even high culture, possible.

Russian fur merchants began to arrive in the 1740s. The coming of the Europeans, as elsewhere in North and South America, had a drastic impact on the Native population. Europeans unwittingly introduced measles, smallpox, and other maladies for which the Natives had no immunity. The introduction of liquor and firearms also speeded the erosion of Natives' traditional lives. In 1741, the year Vitus Bering claimed Alaska for Russia, the Aleut population is thought to have been between 12,000 and 15,000. By 1800 it had dwindled to 2,000. A similar fate befell some other Native groups, such as the Tlingit and Haida of Alaska's Southeast.

There were notable cases of harmony between Natives and newcomers. Contacts with outsiders, at least temporarily, actually enriched the indigenous cultures. On the Southeast coast, for example, the ready availability of iron tools encouraged an expansion of Native woodworking traditions. New wealth created by the fur trade made more frequent and lavish ceremonial feasts, or potlatches, possible.

But the sometimes-violent struggle for control of the region led inevitably to non-Native dominance. Some Russian Orthodox priests and Anglo-American missionaries made sincere, though sometimes misguided, efforts to protect and educate the Natives. Yet in Russian America, as in the Canadian and American West, the commercial drive usually won out. A favorite saying of the rough-and-ready promyshlenniki (Russian fur traders) could just as easily describe the unrestrained conduct of many of Alaska's other foreign visitors: "God is in his heaven, and the tsar is far away."

BAIDARKA: THE UNANGÂX WAY

Aleut kayaker of Unalaska. Drawing by John Webber, 1778.

Today's 8,000 Aleut people descend from hunters who moved from the Alaska mainland into the Aleutian Chain some 4,500 years ago. The volcanic peaks of the Aleutian Islands sweep in a 1,200-mile arc from the western tip of the Alaska Peninsula toward Kamchatka in Siberia along the top of the "Pacific Rim." The name "Alaska" itself may derive from the Aleut word "alaxsxag" or "agunalaksh," meaning either "great land," or more poetically "shores where the sea breaks its back."

Aleutian temperatures are surprisingly mild—the most southerly island lies just north of Seattle's latitude—but violent 125-knot winds, heavy rain, and dense fog are typical. Yet below uninviting skies the ocean abounds with life. This natural wealth drew the Aleuts toward the sea and a seafaring life.

Knowledge of pre-Russian contact Aleut life is sparse, though archaeologists are unearthing more evidence. The word "Aleut" is actually a Russian label. The people called themselves Unangâx (oo-NUNG-ah, "original people"), but under Russian rule they accepted the term Aleut—and Orthodox Christianity, a hallmark of their post-contact identity. In today's climate of heritage revival, "Unangâx" (sing. "Unangan") is increasingly used, though "Aleut" remains common. In many ways the best authority on Aleut folkways is Father Ivan Veniaminov, who worked as a Russian Orthodox priest among the Aleuts in the 1820s and 1830s, leaving detailed and enlightening notes on their culture. The people lived in earthen lodges (called barabaras by the Russians) and mummified and entombed some of their elite dead in caves where volcanic heat aided preservation. Aleut women were remarkable basket makers and seamstresses, weaving elegant watertight containers from island grasses and fashioning all-weather clothing from the skins of birds and marine animals. The men were consummate masters of maritime hunting, perfectly adapted to their marine world. In this they exemplified the qualities that strike us today as so remarkable about Alaska's Native peoples: their ingenious, creative use of the environment and their harmonious adjustment to nature's rhythms.

Using harpoons and wearing steam-bent visors made of carved and painted driftwood and fitted with amulets designed to ensure hunting success, Aleut paddlers traveled hundreds of miles in skin-covered kayaks that the Russians called baidarkas. Early visitors marveled at the seaworthiness and sheer grace of these boats, which Aleut boys learned to make and maneuver from the age of six or seven. "If perfect symmetry, smoothness, and proportion constitute beauty, they are beautiful," wrote 18th-century traveler Martin Sauer. Russian naval officer Gavriil Davydov observed, "The one-man Aleut baidarka is so narrow and light that hardly anyone else would dare to put to sea in them, although the Aleuts fear no storm when in them."

Aleuts made their boats watertight by fastening their gutskin parkas to the gunwales of their vessels—a method still used by modern kayakers. Their quarry were Steller's sea lions, seals, sea otters, the now-extinct Steller's sea cow, and (using poisoned harpoon points) small whales. And they harvested salmon, halibut, and other marine life.

Ironically, the hunters' prowess worked to their disadvantage after Russian discovery. Siberian fur traders used them as forced labor to do their hunting for them, holding their families hostage. Aleut warriors resisted, but arrows and amulets couldn't prevail against firearms. The three-hatch baidarka was devised to enhance control over the hunters: an armed Russian overseer occupied the lead kayak's middle seat in every hunting party. By the 1830s, Aleut paddlers—aided by transport on ships— traveled as far afield as California in relentless pursuit of the sea otter. Some hunters were also resettled north to the Pribilof Islands to harvest fur seals for their Russian overlords.

Aleut hunter with bentwood visor. Drawing by John Webber, 1778.

INUA: THE ESKIMO WORLD

Eskimos of the Gulf of Kotzebue. Drawing by Louis Choris, 1816–17.

Eskimos, the last of Alaska's Native people to migrate from Siberia, belong to a hunting culture spanning the Arctic from Siberia to Greenland. They occupy, in fact, the largest geographical expanse of any of the earth's cultures. The name "Eskimo" evokes many stereotypes—ice-hewn igloos, for instance, sometimes built by Greenlanders and the Canadian Inuit but not (except in traveling emergencies) by Alaska Natives. In truth, the term encompasses diverse ways of life reflecting the different conditions under which Eskimos live. Alaska's Eskimos belong to two distinct language groups. Above the northern shore of Norton Sound live the Iñupiat; south of that line Yup'ik is spoken, from the sprawling Yukon-Kuskokwim Delta down to Bristol Bay and the Alaska Peninsula. A small, distinct subgroup known as Siberian Yupik—walrus and whale hunters with kinship ties to Russian Natives—live mainly on St. Lawrence Island in the Bering Sea. These Eskimo subcultures share many customs yet are different in important ways.

The Iñupiat people of the High Arctic live half the year or more under dark and frigid conditions, yet have evolved a hunting and whaling culture suited to their daunting environment. The Yup'ik Eskimos live in a less severe, subarctic setting, rich in sea mammals, salmon, waterfowl, and herds of inland caribou.

The early Eskimos' weapons and hunting kit, fashioned from bone, ivory, and driftwood and engraved with magic images, reflected their belief that animals wish to be killed by beautiful tools. Despite the stark appearance of their world—the treeless landscape and icy waters—resources were plentiful to the practiced eye. Roaming inland—also home to Athabascan Indians with whom they traded and often warred—they took caribou, bear, and other land animals. In the Yukon-Kuskokwim Delta, the Yup'ik established many inland settlements.

Men fished, hunted waterfowl, and harpooned seals from slender kayaks. Wider beamed umiaks—open-hulled vessels covered in walrus hide—carried hunting parties in pursuit of whales and ivory-tusked walrus. An Eskimo specialty, especially among the Iñupiat, whale hunting required high levels of community planning and sharing. Membership in a whaling crew brought special honor and, following a successful hunt, the meat was divided among all members of the community.

Winter's enforced leisure produced a rich ceremonial life, centered in the qasgiq (men's house), an earthen and driftwood bath-house and hunter's lodge that doubled as a meeting place for community rituals. In the Eskimo world, humans, animals, and even stones have an inner soul, or inua, with the power to transform into other life forms. A man might become a seal, or a walrus a man. A dead creature's spirit remained alive in the bladder, carefully preserved by the hunter until—in the bladder festival—it was returned to the sea to be reborn in another animal.

Whalers invaded west Alaskan waters in the 1840s; traders brought firearms, liquor, illness, and the cash economy; and gold was found at Nome in 1898. By the turn of the century, each sizable settlement included a modern school and white schoolmaster. Today, the old ways survive, but the modern hunter prefers the snowmobile and outboard engine to the sled or kayak. Yet the spirit world remains a powerful force for traditional Eskimos, and endures in their graceful bone and ivory carvings, wooden masks, and other Native arts.

ALASKA'S ATHABASCAN PEOPLE

Athabascan man of Fort Yukon. Photo by E.W. Nelson, about 1877.

Alaska's Athabascan Natives, scattered mainly across the Interior, occupy a vast homeland that also extends south to Cook Inlet's shores, part of the Kenai Peninsula, and eastward to the Copper River basin and Canada. Bows and arrows for hunting, snowshoes, fringed and beaded moose and caribou hide clothing, and canoes and utensils made of birch bark were hallmarks of their traditional culture. Athabascans are divided into various regional groups—the Tanaina of Cook Inlet, the Tanana and Koyukon of the central Interior, and the Ahtna of the Copper River country, for instance. (The Eyak, a small group related to Athabascans but influenced by Tlingit culture, live in the Copper River delta.) Their diverse languages, part of the same broad Na-Dene speech group, belong to the same language family as the Southwest's Navajo and Apache. Mainly nomadic, Athabascan hunters and trappers followed moose, caribou, and other mammals of the taiga steppe, muskeg flats, and conifer and birch forests lying north of the coastal mountains. Along major rivers and tributaries, they lived a seminomadic life, setting up summer fish camps to harvest the rich salmon runs swimming upriver from the sea.

Spartan survivalists habituated to Alaska's severe Interior winters, Athabascan peoples were known for exceptional strength, resourcefulness, and stamina. They traveled light in small groups, on a moment's notice, following the migration paths of their game. Their caches, elevated log boxes to store food and gear, are icons of wild Alaska. In summer they lived in easily collapsible bark houses, and in winter built semi-underground dwellings or used domed lodges of moose or caribou hide. Caribou were as important to Alaska's Athabascans as bison were to southern Plains Indians, and their hunting methods were highly efficient. In autumn, herds were driven into staked barriers equipped with snares, or funneled into corrals where 20 hunters could kill hundreds of animals—several months' supply of food, skins, horn, and bones.

When Russian agents established an Interior fur trade in southwest Alaska in the 1820s and 1830s, many Athabascans of the region became contract trappers employed by the Russian-American Company. It was an entrepreneurial way of life for which their traditions of mobility and solitary hardiness prepared them well.

In the enforced leisure of winter, they held potlatches—ceremonial feasts to mark important events such as deaths, births, and marriages.

For Athabascans, as for other Alaska Natives, all creation was a spirit realm in which the human and non-human were one. Elaborate rituals and taboos governed the use of nature's resources. There was a formalized reverence for the earth and its life forms. Nature in the Interior was less generous than along the coast; resources were scarce, starvation was possible in lean years, and the spirit of every animal killed demanded its due of gratitude and honor. Tradition required, for instance, that each animal be ritually fed after being killed. Despite Russian Orthodox, Protestant, and Catholic missionary activity, ancient beliefs survive even today among many villagers. "They believe everything has spirits," writes a contemporary Eskimo neighbor. "The land, the leaves, water, everything… [Their] view is that this is a watchful world, and the world knows human action. So you have to be really careful what you do, or else there will be consequences."

People of the Rain Forest: Tlingit, Haida, and Tsimshian

Cape Fox village near Wrangell. Photo by Edward Curtis, 1899.

The gray-green islands, misty fjords, and spruce and cedar rainforests of Alaska's Southeast are home to three Indian groups: the Tlingit, Haida, and Tsimshian. At the time of Russian contact (and today), the Tlingit were most numerous of these Native people, their villages and fishing camps strewn among the islands and along the narrow shore from Yakutat Bay south to today's Prince of Wales Island. The Haida, renowned builders of seagoing dugout canoes, were clustered on the (now Canadian) Queen Charlotte Islands—today called Haida Gwaii—and the south end of Prince of Wales Island. The Tsimshian were last to arrive in Alaska. Seeking better living conditions, 823 Tsimshian moved from British Columbia to Alaska's Annette Island near Ketchikan in 1887, led by Anglican lay minister William Duncan. Today about 1,000 Alaska Tsimshian live there in the village of Metlakatla, which is Alaska's only Indian reservation.

Alaska's linguistically and ethnically distinct but culturally similar Southeast Indian peoples lived in an area blessed with a mild, maritime climate and plentiful food. The abundant salmon made possible a life of relative wealth and leisure. They evolved elaborate rituals and kinship systems, and the arts flourished, creating the most complex Native American cultures and societies north of Mexico's Mayan and Aztec civilizations. This sophistication was amply reflected in their richly carved cedar artifacts, such as ceremonial masks, house posts, colorful totem poles, and canoes, and their striking woven hats, baskets, and the celebrated blankets of the Chilkat Tlingit.

A defining tradition of the Southeast peoples was the potlatch, an elaborate ceremonial feast involving dancing, storytelling, and gift-giving by the hosts. Potlatches were held to celebrate major life events and to validate the social status of the hosts. Occasionally slaves, commercially valuable commodities, were sacrificed or set free as ultimate proof of the host's wealth, or highly valued "coppers"—shield-like sheets of pounded copper—might be broken or destroyed.

Outsiders considered the potlatch, like masks and totems, evidence of heathenism—something to be eradicated. In fact, the potlatch tradition embodied an important logic, for it reinforced the vital fabric of social roles and authority patterns that held Southeast Coast cultures together. Efforts by whites to uproot potlatching by discouraging Native customs or even prohibition (the potlatch was outlawed in neighboring Canada from 1884 to 1951) served to erode community bonds and, ultimately, cultural vigor. Adding to the impact of liquor, firearms, and new diseases, the traditional ways of the coastal peoples rapidly deteriorated. In recent decades the potlatch has returned and Native language-recovery programs have blossomed, contributing to a renewal of cultural prosperity. Today, new generations are rediscovering a heritage that was almost extinguished.

Crossroads of Cultures: Alutiiq/Sugpiaq Heritage in Alaska's Gulf

"We are Alutiiq! We are Alutiiq!" In Kodiak's new Alutiiq Museum, youthful dancers in ethnic regalia proudly intoned the chant during a performance shortly after its 1995 opening. Their verbal tattoo proclaimed the rise of a newly minted sense of Native community among residents of the Gulf of Alaska. Was it a renaissance of ancient heritage or an invention of modern politics? Or both?

Until the 1980s ethnologists usually distinguished three broad Alaska Native cultures: Unangâx/Aleut, Eskimo, and Indian. Yet civil rights ideals of the 1960s—combined with the discovery of Alaskan oil and Native land claims legislation (see page 120 and 124)—converged to kindle a Native politics in a new key, including on Kodiak Island, Prince William Sound, and the Kenai and Alaska Peninsulas. Today, knowledgeable observers often add "Alutiiq" or "Sugpiaq" (or both) to the inventory of Alaska's broadly defined Native groups.

This story has a richly braided background. In the 1700s, Russian colonizers imported the Siberian word "Aleut" (Aleuty) as a catch-all name for Natives they subjugated in the Aleutian Islands and Alaska's Pacific Gulf (including the Kodiak Archipelago). Though people of these two areas spoke different languages and often fought, the people eventually accepted the label, along with Russian Orthodox Christianity. Many Russian traders married Native wives, producing a sizable "creole" (kreoly) population with mixed ancestry and Russian surnames. The name "Aleut," Orthodox Christianity, and Russian ancestry became signatures of identity. After America's 1867 purchase of Alaska, the population was leavened by influxes of Americans and Europeans to work in whaling and fisheries. Many married local wives, yielding a host of European surnames. According to late Kodiak Judge Roy Madsen, whose father was Danish, "They flavored the mix, like herbs applied to a dish after the salt and pepper."

Meanwhile, linguists determined that the speech of most Gulf Natives derived from the Yup'ik languages of Bering Sea Eskimos, but was entirely different from that of Aleutian islanders, so ethnologists decided they were "Pacific Eskimo" rather than Aleut.

(More localized ethnic modifiers were widely used, too, especially "Koniag" and "Chugach.") Generally, though, local people rejected "Eskimo" and preferred "Aleut" (or "Russian" or just "American"). Anthropologists conceded that their folkways shared more with Aleuts than Eskimos; to confound things, scholars noticed that some of their art forms overlapped with Southeast Alaska's Tlingit Indians. Centuries of cross-fertilization created, as Madsen observed, a "heterogeneous culture. . . mixed, mingled, blended and combined with those of many other cultures. . . "

The Alaska Native Claims Settlement Act of 1971 (ANCSA) (see page 136) became a catalyst for an experiment to fuse these sundry traditions into a shared sense of "Alutiiq" ethnicity. This federal law resolved Native land claims to enable construction of a pipeline to move Arctic oil to Alaska's Gulf. It awarded Alaska's Native groups, collectively, 44 million acres of land and $962.5 million, and established regional economic development corporations to manage the wealth for Native shareholders (defined as people of at least one-quarter Alaska Native ancestry). Overnight, it created ethnically defined, regional shareholder constituencies with varying financial and political interests. Across Alaska, Native leaders began to craft strategies that promoted stockholders' interests. They quickly recognized the psychological importance of shared heritage for galvanizing and empowering constituents—not least in Alaska's Gulf, with its mosaic of influences and sometimes absent or confused sense of Native ethnicity. In the 1970s, recalls Gordon Pullar, little Native heritage awareness existed in Kodiak; when named president of the Kodiak Area Native Association in 1983, he himself "had little idea of what it meant to be Alutiiq." Enabled by ANCSA and federal grants, local leaders and curators— some fashioning new Native identities themselves—launched heritage projects in the 1980s: museums, exhibitions, archaeological digs, and school and language-revival programs. Damages from the 1989 *Exxon Valdez* oil tanker spill financed the Alutiiq Museum. The Alutiiq identity project and its semantics are still evolving. Indeed, the (evidently pre-Russian) name "Sugpiaq" (meaning "the real people") increasingly rivals "Alutiiq" as a preferred name in some circles. Still, it appears that Kodiak's heritage-builders have made a case for an imagined Alutiiq community in Alaska's Pacific Gulf. There's perhaps irony, though, in the fact that "Alutiiq" is Yup'ik (Sugtestun) rendition of that old Russian import "Aleut."

St. Michael's Cathedral and Russian-American Company buildings, Sitka, late 180-

RUSSIAN AMERICA:
THE FORGOTTEN
FRONTIER

Promyshlenniki and the Russian Fur Trade

Old Russian block house at Sitka,
with "Baranov's Castle" in background which burned in 1894.

The arrival of the first Europeans in Alaska, the Russians, grew largely out of their fur trading operations in Siberia. Trappers and traders called promyshlenniki began to extend European influence east from Moscow and Kiev toward Siberia in the late 1500s. For adventurers and entrepreneurs, Central Asia and Siberia represented the Russian frontier of the day, a land of opportunity similar to the American and Canadian frontiers of the 1700s and 1800s.

Like the American mountain men and French-Canadian voyageurs, the promyshlenniki sought furs that commanded dazzling prices in Europe and, especially, China. Sometimes they trapped the fur-bearing animals themselves; in Siberia sable was the most valuable. More often, they extracted tribute in the form of furs from the Asiatic tribes they encountered—distant relatives of the Native peoples they would later find in Alaska. This system, in which hostages were taken to enforce the tribute, later became a model for Russian operations in Alaska.

Pushing ever eastward as regions were trapped out, by the 1690s the promyshlenniki reached the Kamchatka Peninsula on Siberia's Pacific coast. The imperial Russian government and the Russian Orthodox Church extended their influence along trails and waterways opened up by these pioneers, especially during the reign of Tsar Peter the Great between 1689 and 1725. The tsarist government appointed agents to collect a 10 percent tax on the furs. In strategic places it established ostrogs, or citadels—fortified trading posts, which were isolated wilderness camps. In 1726, Okhotsk, Russia's most important Pacific port until the early 1800s, was a tiny cluster of log sheds and dwellings, a chapel, and only 10 or 11 Russian households. (Later, St. Paul Harbor on Alaska's Kodiak Island [founded in 1792] and New Archangel—today's Stika, founded in 1804 and center of Russia's American operations after 1808—were established as such remote outposts.)

In January 1725, shortly before his own death, Tsar Peter commissioned a naval expedition to explore Pacific waters north and east of Kamchatka. The emperor's motives were more scientific and political than economic. He wanted to know if Asia and North America were joined by land, to determine the extent of Spain's control in the Pacific, and to extend Russian power into the New World. But his order would have important economic consequences— it would inaugurate the Alaskan fur trade. Alaska's European discovery was at hand.

First Contacts: The Voyages of Bering and Chirikov

A sea otter. Drawing by John Webber, 1778.

Two ships set sail from the Siberian coast in June 1741 on an expedition commissioned by the Russian government. At the helm of the ill-fated *St. Peter* was Vitus Bering, a 60-year-old Danish captain who had served the tsar's navy since he was 23. The *St. Paul's* master and Bering's second officer was Aleksei Chirikov. Aboard the *St. Peter* rode the temperamental but gifted German naturalist and physician Georg Wilhelm Steller; biologists still refer to "Steller's sea lion," "Steller's jay," "Steller's eider," and "Steller's sea eagle" as a consequence of his fieldwork on the journey.

Bering had sailed these waters before. In 1728 he piloted the *St. Gabriel* through the strait that now bears his name, concluding that Asia and America were not joined. On that voyage, however, he never saw the fog-shrouded Alaska mainland. Disappointed when his findings were not deemed conclusive by European scientists or the Russian government, Bering successfully lobbied for the chance to lead another expedition.

On this second voyage, Bering and Chirikov lost contact in foul weather, never to meet again. Each maintained an eastward course, however, and in July both ships sighted southern Alaska. On July 16, Steller led a landing party on Kayak Island at Cape Saint Elias, just east of Prince William Sound. He quickly gathered a few plants and birds before being ordered back to the ship by Bering. Chirikov had sighted the islands of Southeast Alaska a day earlier, but the two small boats he sent ashore for fresh water never returned to the mother ship. Their fate has remained a mystery.

Their diets short on vitamin C, many of Bering's crew became ill with scurvy—the captain included. Weak and exhausted by years of labor struggling with the imperial bureaucracy, Bering was anxious to get back to Kamchatka before the cold weather began. Instead of wintering in Alaska, as Steller advised, the explorer sailed for home. In heavy seas the *St. Peter* ran aground on a rocky island off the Siberian coast, since known as Bering Island. Twenty of the stranded sailors died of scurvy, including Bering, on December 8, 1741. Those remaining survived with Steller's medical care and eventually built a 40-foot boat from the wreck of the *St. Peter*. They finally reached Kamchatka in the spring. Chirikov had already made a safe return in the previous October.

Bering's voyage not only laid the basis for Russian claims to Alaska but also opened the fur trade. His crews brought back many pelts, among them 800 sea otter skins, more prized even than sable on Chinese markets because of their plush density. The fur-trading promyshlenniki immediately began to outfit trips to the Aleutians, and the fur rush was on. By the late 1700s—the era of Catherine the Great—the Russian fur trade became the richest fur enterprise in the world; a single sea otter skin might equal three times a man's yearly income and profits were dazzling—100 percent on the average.

As for the otters, eventually they were hunted to near extinction— by the 1820s sea otters were scarce even as far south as Oregon and California. Harder hit was the "Steller's sea cow," which became extinct by 1768 because the fur traders had hunted them for food. Our only full description of the large, manatee-like beast is Steller's.

In the Russians' Wake:
British and French Explorers

The death of 21 French sailors in rip tides, Lituya Bay, 1786.

For decades following Bering's 1741–42 expedition, Russia enjoyed uncontested control of Alaskan seas, and the lucrative fur trade remained a closely guarded secret. By the 1770s, however, the explorers of other nations began to penetrate the North Pacific. Spain was the first power to encounter Russia in the New World. But ultimately, Russia's greatest challenge came from Britain and the new American republic.

In the late 1770s, British Captain James Cook sailed north under orders to find an ice-free passage from the Pacific to the Atlantic. Along the way he produced the first reliable charts of the Northwest Coast. (Cook's best cartographer was the young William Bligh, later of *Mutiny on the Bounty* notoriety.)

In May 1778, Cook reached the bay since known as Cook Inlet, site of modern Anchorage, noting the region's promise for the fur trade but doubting its value for Britain without discovery of a northern channel.

Searching for just such a passage, he sailed through the Bering Strait, but was stopped by ice in the Chukchi Sea. Turning southward, he charted the Aleutian Islands for two months. He then sailed for Hawaii where he was killed by Polynesian Natives.

Cook's crew returned to Alaska in another futile search for the passage, and as they sailed for England via the China Sea made an astounding discovery. In Canton, they found that sea otter furs fetched astronomical prices. A ship's officer wrote the "rage with which our seamen were possessed to return to Cook's River (Cook Inlet) and buy another cargo of skins at one time was not far short of mutiny."

The word was out; others soon followed. In a measure of sea otter skins' value, New England trader Robert Gray sold his sloop *Adventure* to the Spanish Captain Bodega y Quadra for 75 prime skins. But the most famous of those sailing in Cook's wake was George Vancouver, a veteran of Cook's last voyage.

In a four-year expedition between 1791 and 1795, Vancouver charted the Inside Passage, and became the first European to sight from Cook Inlet "distant stupendous mountains covered with snow"—now known as Mount Foraker and nearby Denali, the continent's highest peak.

By 1805, at least 200 European scientific and commercial voyages had been made up the Northwest Coast by the Russians, British, Americans, Spanish, and French. Most tragic of the early expeditions was that of Jean François Galaup de la Pérouse, master of the French vessel *Boussole*, which visited Lituya Bay near Yakutat in July 1786. In a humbling display of nature's power, two of the ship's small boats attempting to chart the bay's mouth were caught in violent rip tides, killing all 21 crewmen. Later on the ill-starred voyage, the expedition's second-in-command and nine others were killed by Natives in Samoa. Their troubles did not end there. La Pérouse, along with the *Boussole* and his remaining crew, disappeared in a 1788 typhoon in the southwest Pacific.

MALASPINA AND THE
SPANISH INCURSIONS

"Return of the Stolen Trousers." Drawing by José Cardero, 1791–92.

The luster of Spain's American empire—created in the age of Columbus, Cortés, and Pizarro—had tarnished considerably by the time the Russians landed in Alaska in 1741. Still, Spain's proud tradition compelled her to contest all rival claims to America's Pacific shore. From her naval base at San Blas in Baja California, Spain sent 13 voyages northward between 1774 and 1793 under such commanders as Bodega y Quadra, Arteaga, Martínez, Lopez de Haro, and Malaspina.

Some expeditions pushed as far as Prince William Sound and the Aleutians. Spanish charts of Alaska's waters and fjords were often more thorough and precise than those produced by Russian or British cartographers. This helps explain why so many Spanish place names stuck: present-day Ketchikan, for instance, is located on Revillagigedo Island, named for a viceroy of New Spain, and the site of modern Valdez (today pronounced val-DEEZ by Alaskans) was christened Puerto de Valdés by Captain Salvador Fidalgo in 1790.

Though Spain never controlled Alaskan soil, Russian-Spanish tensions had far-reaching consequences for the North Pacific region. Partly out of fear of Russian expansion southward, the Spanish moved into what was known as Upper California, where they founded missions and presidios in San Diego (1769), Monterey (1770), and San Francisco (1776).

Among the most notable Spanish incursions was the expedition of Captain Alejandro Malaspina, which sailed from Cádiz, Spain, in July 1789. Malaspina's ships, the *Descubierta* (Discovery) and *Atrevida* (Daring) were lavishly outfitted, and the Spanish crown hoped the expedition's scientific achievements would exceed those of the great British navigator, Captain James Cook. After two years mapping the shores of South America and Mexico, Malaspina received orders to head for Alaska to search for the fabled Northwest Passage, believed to link the Pacific and Atlantic oceans at the top of the globe. The mission led him to Yakutat Bay in June 1791. "Great was the joy of the commander and all the officers," wrote Tomás de Suria, the ship's artist, "because they believed… that this might be the much-desired and sought-for strait." Two weeks of exploration, however, produced only disappointment. Malaspina named the inlet Bahia de Desengaño ("Disenchantment Bay") when he discovered that it ended abruptly at the face of a great glacier.

Though he had failed in his major purpose, Malaspina remained in the area for over a month, charting the coasts and collecting scientific information. The immense Malaspina Glacier, Alaska's largest, is named in his honor. His stay at Yakutat also produced some wonderful drawings by de Suria and two other ship's artists, José Cardero and Felipe Bauzá. At one point a sailor's trousers were stolen by Tlingit residents, but a levelheaded chief prevented the affair from escalating by returning the pants, an incident captured in a drawing by Cardero.

In a melancholy postscript, upon his return to Europe in 1794 Malaspina became entangled in intrigues at the Spanish court, was imprisoned for eight years, then banished from the country. The journals of the man sent to outdo Cook lay forgotten in the archives until resentments faded, and they were finally published in 1885.

LORD OF ALASKA:
ALEXANDER BARANOV

Alexander Baranov

Alexander Andreyevich Baranov was a "doer," just the sort of man demanded by the unforgiving conditions of the Great Land.

Hired in 1790 to manage Russian America's dominant fur trading company owned by Grigori Shelikov, the 43-year-old Baranov seemed an unlikely choice. His own Siberian fur business had recently failed. But his charisma, aggressiveness, and tough—sometimes brutal—political skills proved indispensable to the survival and expansion of Russia's American empire. Within seven years he eliminated all competitors and secured the Alaska coast—from the Aleutian Islands to Yakutat—for Shelikov's firm; renamed the Russian-American Company (RAC), Tsar Paul I granted it an Alaskan trade monopoly in 1799.

Learning to handle an Aleut baidarka and navigate a seagoing sloop, he established a citadel at remote Sitka Bay in 1799 and, in 1804, reestablished the post following its destruction by Tlingit warriors.

From his own small kremlin, Sitka's Castle Hill, Baranov ruled like a now severe, now enlightened despot with a practical knack for making the colony prosper. He encouraged marriage between European men and Native women. His own Native wife, Anna, bore him a son and daughter. The settlement's need for clerks and artisans led him to provide basic schooling for creole (Russian-Native) children and, in gifted cases, technical training in Siberia. One colony youngster later became a brigadier general in the Russian army.

Baranov was equally pragmatic in dealing with foreign intruders. Lacking military support to exclude British and American vessels from Alaskan waters, he made a virtue of necessity by cultivating cordial relations with foreign captains. Boston traders—notably the enterprising Irishman Joseph O'Cain—supplied Baranov's outpost with food and sold company furs in southern China, where Russians were forbidden to trade.

Baranov's lavish, alcoholic receptions for foreigners became legend. "They all drink an astonishing quantity, Baranov not excepted," reported American captain John Ebbets. "It is no small tax on the health of a person trying to do business with him." His reputation as host spread to Hawaii and even New England, where Washington Irving described him as a "rough, rugged, hard-drinking old Russian; somewhat of a soldier, somewhat of a trader, above all a boon companion."

Yet Baranov had a darker side. He had a stormy relationship with the Russian Church, which criticized his sometimes-abusive treatment of Natives and RAC workers. Arthritis became an excuse for heavy private drinking, and the bleak isolation of Alaska's winters drove him to fits of depression. The worst came in 1809, after nine disgruntled colonists who considered him a tyrant plotted to murder him and his family. The plot was foiled, but Baranov sent his family to Kodiak, submitted his resignation, and passed the winter in an alcoholic stupor. After two intended replacements died en route to Alaska, however, Baranov declared that God had ordained that he continue as governor.

Reinvigorated, he directed the company to its most profitable years to date in 1813 and 1814. When he finally retired at age 71, Russian influence in the North Pacific stretched from Siberia to an RAC farming station at Fort Ross in northern California. Yet his last few years as company director were not happy. Revenues were uneven, there were rumors of his physical and mental decline, and he was accused (falsely) of profiting at RAC expense. Neither Baranov—nor his successors—solved the problem of properly supplying Russia's remote colony with food. In 1818 he was replaced as chief manager by the naval officer Leontii Hagemeister.

The "Lord of Alaska," the man who more than any other helped Russia tap the New World's riches, died of fever aboard the ship *Kutuzov* on April 12, 1819, en route to St. Petersburg, off the coast of Java.

APOSTLE OF ALASKA:
FATHER IVAN VENIAMINOV

St. Michael's Cathedral, Sitka. LaRoche photo, late 1800s.

Near the Sitka waterfront stand two wooden structures that powerfully recall Alaska's Russian heritage: the Russian Bishop's House, completed in 1842, and the onion-domed St. Michael's Cathedral, first dedicated in 1848. Both are products of a man whose work as a religious leader, craftsman, and scholar has been as enduring as the buildings themselves: Father Ivan Veniaminov.

Veniaminov was born in Siberia in 1797, the son of a church caretaker. Young Ivan attended the Russian Orthodox seminary in Irkutsk, where he was not only the outstanding scholar of his class but displayed a restless interest in mechanical crafts. From a local artisan he learned the art of clock making. (Later, as Bishop of Alaska, he built the belfry clock of St. Michael's.) In 1821 the young priest was ordained and, three years later, he traveled with his wife, son, and elderly mother as a missionary to the east Aleutian Island of Unalaska.

Tall and athletic, Veniaminov had the practical genius of a Benjamin Franklin. He immediately established a sympathetic rapport with his Native parishioners. Using his craftsman's skills, the artisan priest set to work on his own house, furniture, and a church. In the process he taught woodworking, blacksmithing, and brickmaking to Native apprentices. An amateur scientist, he compiled observations on local plant and animal life, the weather, and tides.

Unlike some later American missionaries who tried to suppress Native dialects and customs, Veniaminov respected local traditions—at least when they did not directly contradict Orthodox teachings—and taught that Natives must receive Christian doctrine in their own tongue. A gifted linguist, Father Veniaminov preached in Aleut, prepared (with the help of Aleut headman Ivan Pan'kov) an Aleut dictionary, grammar, and primer, and laid the foundations of literacy among the Aleut people.

In 1834 he moved to Sitka, where he did similar work among the Tlingit people, winning their trust by inoculating them against a smallpox epidemic in 1836. Among his greatest achievements was his *Notes on the Islands of Unalaska District*, a treasure of information on the early Aleut and Tlingit cultures. A tireless traveler, in 1838 he journeyed to California's Fort Ross and San Francisco Bay to inspect Church affairs and Catholic missions.

Word of Veniaminov's labors reached St. Petersburg, and in 1841 he traveled there and was named "Innocent, Bishop of Kamchatka, the Kurile, and the Aleutian Islands." The caretaker's son even had an audience with Tsar Nicholas. Shortly thereafter the Bishop's House and Cathedral were built in Sitka.

St. Michael's was destroyed by fire in 1966, but its icons and other artifacts were saved, and the church was faithfully rebuilt according to the original plans. The Bishop's House, which functioned as a school and chapel as well as Veniaminov's residence, has been meticulously restored by the National Park Service as one of the focal points of Sitka National Historical Park.

In 1868 Veniaminov was called back to Russia and named Metropolitan of Moscow in 1867, the primate of Russia's Church. He held the post until his death in 1879; he was canonized as St. Innocent in 1977. Following the American purchase in 1867, many observers forecast the demise of Russian Orthodox Christianity in Alaska. Today, however, Russian Orthodoxy remains strong among many Natives.

Yankee Whalers

Whale in position for stripping, Tyee, Alaska, late 1800s.

Decades before the United States bought Alaska, New England whalers carried Yankee commercialism deep into Russia's New World domain. Before kerosene and electricity, whale oil (rendered from whale blubber in massive iron kettles) was prized as lamp oil. Baleen, a flexible comb-like material that enables non-toothed whale species to strain their food (krill, plankton) from sea water, was fashioned into women's corset and men's collar stays, umbrella ribbing, buggy whips, and skirt hoops.

Both products—like the walrus oil and ivory that Alaskan whalers also sought—were enormously profitable, enriching the merchant princes of New Bedford, New London, Nantucket, and Sag Harbor a world away in New England.

In 1835 American and French ships sailed north from Hawaii to the Gulf of Alaska in search of blubber-laden right whales, whose numbers already had been severely reduced in the Atlantic and southern Pacific oceans. Within the gulf, an upwelling from the ocean floor and the warm Kuro Siwo, or Japanese current, created rich feeding grounds for the right whales.

In 1846, the heyday of square-rigger whaling, 292 ships operated off Kodiak Island. At roughly the same time, Yankee vessels ventured north of the Aleutians, through the Bering Strait and into Arctic waters. There they made contact with resident Eskimos, who were skilled at hunting the bowhead whale—even richer in oil and baleen than the right whale. (The pursuit of stronger and faster humpbacks had to await the advent of harpoon cannons and steam whaling ships.)

On occasion, whalers were trapped in the Arctic pack ice; ships were crushed and crewmen perished. But the whalers—a mix of New England masters and seamen, Europeans, Native Americans and African Americans, and Polynesians—were relentless hunters. With the advent of the harpoon gun in the 1860s, whaling became coldly efficient and even more devastating to animal populations.

By 1865 the right whale was rarely sighted, confirming a Nor'west seaman's prediction two decades before that "the poor whale is doomed to utter extermination, or at least, so near to it that too few will remain to tempt the cupidity of man."

The price of whale oil plunged after the 1859 discovery of petroleum in Pennsylvania, but baleen remained valuable. Such was the industry's importance to New England's economy during the Civil War that, late in the conflict, the Confederacy dispatched the warship *Shenandoah* under Captain James Waddell to destroy the American whaling fleet. Setting out from Australia, Waddell and the *Shenandoah* crew destroyed whalers across the Pacific. In the Bering Strait alone, they captured and burned 20 whale ships—unaware that the South had surrendered before they completed their mission.

Whaling was, for the most part, hardly romantic. But in the human imagination, whaling took on an epic aura, as reflected in Herman Melville's *Moby Dick*. Some of that romance lives on in Eskimos' ivory carving and the decorative etchings of ivory scrimshaw. Angokwazhuk, or "Happy Jack," a turn-of-the-century Cape Nome carver, forged the elements of today's Eskimo carving style by combining ancient Native motifs and modern whalers' scrimshaw.

Yet today's artistry conceals a poignant past. Firearms brought new levels of efficiency and waste to the hunt. When whales could not be found, the guns were turned on walrus. Between 1860 and 1880, white and Native hunters slaughtered 200,000 walruses.

Stampeders climb the summit of Chilkoot Pass. Cantwell photo, 1898.

EXPLORERS, ADVENTURERS, AND NATURALISTS: AMERICA'S NEW FRONTIER

SEWARD'S FOLLY

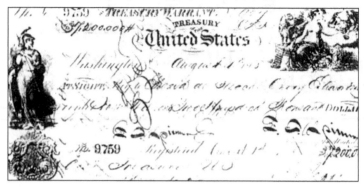

U.S. treasury warrant used for Alaska's purchase in 1867.

Russia's interest in its only overseas colony waned as the Russian-American Company's hunters depleted the once-abundant sea otter. While company visionaries sometimes dreamed of capturing Chinese and Japanese markets and making the Pacific into a "Russian lake," the otter trade was the key to Russia's presence in the area. Russia was really a continental, not a maritime, power. At most, only about 800 Eurasian Russians ever lived in Alaska at any given time, and the RAC was vitally dependent on Native and Russian-Native (kreoly, or "creole") hunters, navigators, clerks, and craftsmen for its overextended operations. Russia's humiliation by Britain and France in the Crimean War (1853–1855), at the other end of her empire, revealed that she was the most economically and socially backward of Europe's great powers. That shocking defeat fueled the government's desire to restructure its operations and consider selling off Alaska. An 1858 treaty with China opened the rich Amur Basin in east Asia to Russian exploitation; it was a more accessible and lucrative alternative to Alaska. As St. Petersburg turned to economizing, modernizing, and streamlining to reclaim its great power status, such far-flung operations as Alaska were deemed expendable.

In 1857 the tsar's brother, the Grand Duke Constantine, urged sale of the region to the United States which, after its defeat of Mexico in 1848 and annexation of California, seemed fated to dominate the Pacific. The outbreak of the American Civil War in

1861 forestalled talks on the issue but following the conflict the time seemed right to open negotiations.

In 1866 Tsar Alexander II instructed his ambassador to Washington, Baron Edouard de Stoeckl, to begin immediate talks with U.S. Secretary of State William H. Seward, an enthusiastic advocate of America's manifest destiny—the then-fashionable notion that the nation had a God-given mission to control the entire Pacific coast.

A selling price of $7.2 million—about two cents an acre—was agreed upon. Seward was eager to buy, and Stoeckl was a wily bargainer—the tsar would have accepted $5 million. The U.S. Senate quickly ratified the treaty on April 4, 1867. No one, incidentally, thought to consult representatives of the Native people, who obviously had staked out the territory long before Russia.

American troops relieved Russian forces at the colonial capital of Sitka that October amid vigorous press and congressional debate over the wisdom of the purchase. Angry editorials denounced the acquisition of apparently worthless real estate. Some ridiculed the agreement as "Seward's folly," and Alaska was caricatured as "Seward's icebox" and "Walrussia."

Horace Greeley, the famous editor of the *New York Herald* best remembered for his admonition, "go west, young man," evidently did not wish American youth to go northwest. He advised any European government interested in dumping unwanted wasteland to contact Seward without delay. Some people, however, saw shimmering dollar signs beneath the northern lights, and Seward's supporters were convinced he had struck a great bargain. In fact, most American newspapers and business leaders supported the purchase. Some enthusiasts cited Alaska's potential mineral wealth—gold fever was already well advanced as the result of the recent California bonanza.

The Russians had discovered small amounts of gold on the Kenai Peninsula in the 1850s, but in truth, few Americans knew anything specific about Alaska. The Russians themselves had never explored much of the Interior. Even Baranof Island, the site of Russia's colonial capital, had not been thoroughly mapped. At the time of its American purchase, Alaska was not only bolshaia zeml'a, the Great Land, it was terra incognita as well.

Pursuing Manifest Destiny

Alaskan explorer Lt. Henry T. Allen (center), U.S. Army, 1885.

At the time of its sale to the United States, Alaska was largely a mysterious treasure. The coastal fringes of the Great Land had been charted in the late 1700s by Russian, British, and Spanish navigators. But few early visitors ventured up the wild rivers into the forbidding Interior. Even the knowledge of Russian-American Company officials was based mainly on the reports of Natives.

Only after the American purchase in 1867 did science begin to discern the bare contours of Alaska's mountains, rivers, and great tundra steppe. American William Healy Dall—zoologist, ethnologist, and scientific jack-of-all-trades—was the best informed of the early investigators. On behalf of the Smithsonian Institution and other government agencies, he made several visits to coastal Alaska.

Though occasionally wrong, Dall was a painstaking observer and classifier in the best hard-edged tradition of Victorian science—and a prolific publisher who achieved a worldwide reputation. "Dall's porpoise" and "Dall's sheep" are but two of the many Alaskan species named in his honor.

Though hardly less knowledgeable than Dall, Ivan Petroff embodied a more roguish and romantic approach. The Russian-born vagabond joined the U.S. Army in the 1860s, deserted twice, and became a research specialist on the Alaska history project of Hubert Howe Bancroft, a San Francisco book dealer who published an early and influential multi-volume history of western North America.

Though not a scientist, on the strength of his Russian skills and research experience Petroff was chosen to conduct the 1880 federal census of Alaska's population and resources. He traveled far up the Yukon River, then swung southwest along the Kuskokwim River, and, finally, south to Kodiak Island. The trip generated a trove of information that, while sometimes unreliable and even deliberately falsified, was a major achievement for the day. For the first time, the world had a general idea of the physical features of Alaska's Interior, as well as the size of its population.

Lt. Henry Allen of Kentucky, an 1882 West Point graduate, accomplished the most stunning exploration feat of Alaska's early American era. Despite several attempts, no one had reached the headwaters of the Copper River, which cuts through the rugged Chugach Mountains to flow into the Gulf of Alaska. Allen's boyish face masked a steel determination, and on March 29, 1885, with several companions he began his assault.

The river was so swift and jammed with rocks and ice that the group soon abandoned most of its provisions, resolving to live from the land. In the process they nearly starved, for game was scarce. In sourdough lingo it was a "hungry country." Surviving on roots and the occasional rabbit they eventually encountered an Ahtna Native leader named Nikolai who acted as guide and liaison with other chiefs as they made their way north.

Allen's party finally crossed the Copper River's headwaters, then descended the Tanana River to the Yukon, and traveled downriver to the Bering Sea—an amazing 1,500-mile journey made in a single season. Allen's commanding officer, General Nelson Miles, called it the greatest act of American exploration since Lewis and Clark crossed the Louisiana Purchase to reach the Pacific.

THE FUR SEAL RUSH

The fur seal harvest, Pribilof Islands, 1888.

During the early years of American rule, furs remained Alaska's richest export item. But the sea otter, so prized when Vitus Bering first reached the area in 1741, had become nearly extinct. Instead, hunters killed the fur seal, whose plush coat became fashionable for the Victorian age's capes and muffs.

Most of Alaska's seals went to the San Francisco–based Alaska Commercial Company, which in 1867 had bought the assets of the Russian-American Company for $155,000—ships, merchandise, and buildings in Sitka and at the Pribilof Island seal rookery. Following America's entry into the area, the hunt's intensity reached such a pitch that authorities feared the seal might go the way of the sea otter. Writer Jack London—a onetime participant in the North Pacific seal rush—captured its aura of greed and reckless cruelty in his novel *The Sea Wolf.*

To halt the seals' decline, the federal government invited bids in 1870 on an exclusive lease for the Pribilof breeding grounds. The Alaska Commercial Company won the lease and for the next 20 years enjoyed a sealing monopoly on the Pribilofs. The company was required to hire local Aleuts to club the seals and skin them—a continuation of Russian practice. For an annual fee of $55,000, Alaska Commercial could slaughter 100,000 animals yearly.

Not surprisingly, the company prospered, and extended its operations to the Aleutians, Kodiak Island, and within the Interior along the Yukon River. The company so dominated area commerce that many white settlers denounced such favoritism and the control of Alaska's economy by "outside interests" (a recurring complaint in years to come).

But the company's apparent sealing monopoly had a major loophole. Excluded from taking seals on the Pribilofs, rival companies in San Francisco and Victoria, British Columbia, began to hunt on the open Pacific, using rifles to kill the animals during spring migrations to their island rookery. The practice was enormously wasteful: many animals died and sank before their carcasses could be recovered. Since female seals nurse only their own offspring, to kill a mother was to kill her pups.

The Alaska Commercial Company lobbied in Washington, D.C., against such open-ocean sealing, and Congress responded by outlawing high-seas hunting in the Bering Sea, where America claimed territorial rights inherited from Russia. That step, however, quickly produced international complications.

The 1886 arrest of the crews of three Canadian sealing vessels by federal authorities flared into an incident involving the United States on one side, and Britain and Canada on the other, who refused to recognize U.S. rights over the Bering Sea. An arbitration court in Paris settled the dispute in 1893 by ruling against America's territorial claim, but also condemning sealing done at sea. Still, the practice continued, and by 1910 only a few thousand seals remained where there once were at least three million. Protected by international agreement since 1911, the northern fur seal populations have since recovered.

The Alaska Commercial Company lost an 1890 bid to renew its Pribilof monopoly. By that time, the market for pelts was in decline. Gold was quickly replacing furs as Alaska's most valuable natural resource.

RUMRUNNERS OF THE INSIDE PASSAGE

The old Totem Bar in Juneau.

Beyond their visions of fulfilling America's manifest destiny, federal officials had no clear idea of how the vast and remote new frontier should or could be governed. For years after Alaska's purchase, they followed a policy of wary trial and error. Yet the region's population was sparse, its economic potential was unclear, and Congress was perhaps wise to proceed with caution.

Until 1884, the armed forces reluctantly shouldered the burden of policing the new territory. The first commandant was 39-year-old General Jefferson C. Davis (no relation to the Confederacy's president). Davis's few hundred troops were thinly sprinkled among Sitka, Fort Wrangell, the Pribilof Islands, and three other tiny garrisons. Morale among officers and enlisted men often ebbed in this strange, distant land of mists and long winter nights.

With its many islands, irregular shorelines, and hidden coves, Alaska was a smuggler's and bootlegger's dream in those early years. The southeastern Panhandle alone contains over 1,000 islands and 13,000 miles of shoreline. To preserve peace among whites and Natives, authorities banned liquor and firearms, but then assigned a skeleton crew of army landlubbers to uphold the law along the seacoast. Within a few years even this tiny force shrank, when troops were tapped for Indian wars in California, Idaho, and Montana.

To make matters worse, whites and Natives had long since learned the art of concocting home brew, or "hootch," a term derived from the Hutsunuwa, or "Hoochenoo," band of Admiralty Island, who were specialists in running illegal stills.

The naturalist John Muir, who visited the area in 1879, described the product as "a vile liquor distilled from a mash made of flour, dried apples, sugar, and molasses, and drunk hot from the still." According to the missionary S. Hall Young, it consisted of "anything that would rot and ferment."

Running rum and guns proved enticingly profitable, especially since the risk was slight. Distances were vast, there were few agents to enforce the law, and smugglers were widely considered heroes by the locals. Members of all trades got into the act: fishermen, cannery workers, whalers, steamer captains—even, on occasion, customs officials themselves. Bootleggers were not always lucky, however, as the story of John Kinkead reveals.

Kinkead was a prominent Sitka resident in the late 1860s and early 1870s, a store owner who served for a time as postmaster and city councilman. His wife, Lizzie, was a temperance advocate and organizer of rallies to combat demon rum. Yet the public thirst for spirits proved so great that, to keep abreast of competitors, Kinkead entered the illegal liquor trade. A customs agent discovered his secret, and his contraband stock was seized. Shortly after the embarrassment, Kinkead moved to Nevada, where he was elected state governor in 1878. Six years later, however, Kinkead won appointment by President Chester Arthur as the region's first governor for a brief one-year stint, during which he urged an end to Alaska's liquor ban.

Despite continuing prohibition, 20 saloons ran more or less openly in the boomtown of Juneau in 1889. After the Klondike gold strike of 1896 and the invasion of tens of thousands of thirsty stampeders, authorities finally conceded that prohibition was impossible. In 1899 Congress acted to substitute a licensing system, despite fierce opposition from one of Alaska's major religious leaders, Sheldon Jackson.

Sheldon Jackson: Christian Soldier of the Great Land

The Rev. Sheldon Jackson, Federal Education Agent for Alaska, 1894.

No man was a bigger force in Americanizing the North than Sheldon Jackson, a feisty and none-too-modest Presbyterian minister. A New Yorker with a Princeton theology degree, Jackson felt divinely called to educate Native children and moderate the clash of whites with Native cultures.

Jackson achieved initial fame in the 1870s founding churches in the Rocky Mountain West. He extended his Christian soldier's vision to Alaska in 1877, founding a mission at Wrangell. Soon afterward his protégé, John Brady, created an industrial boarding school for Natives at Sitka.

Between 1867 and 1884 Alaska had virtually no civil government, and a few hundred soldiers and sailors policed the entire region. Churches filled the public education gap with missionary schools. To showcase the skills inherent in Native arts, Jackson began to collect Eskimo and Indian crafts. (That collection became the core of today's Sheldon Jackson Museum in Sitka.) He became convinced, moreover, that Natives could only be sheltered from liquor and exploitation via wholesale political and educational reform for whites and Natives alike.

First, he argued, civilian government must be introduced to the Far North. Second, a comprehensive educational program for all Alaska's children must be implemented, one combining Christian doctrine and the three "R's" with vocational training. It was a grand vision of a moral empire, but Jackson was able, dynamic, and committed to his righteous cause.

Already prominent in religious circles, he traveled the eastern seaboard, rallying pastors and politicians. He found a key ally in

Senator Benjamin Harrison of Indiana, a fellow Presbyterian and future president. Under Jackson's prodding, Harrison championed a federal law of 1884, the "First Organic Act," that brought civil government to the last frontier.

The act provided for a district governor, but he would be presidentially appointed, not elected locally. Still, the act created a foundation of civil law that paved the way for a second reform of 1912, which made Alaska a U.S. territory with its own legislature.

The Organic Act also provided for public education. Jackson himself was named federal education agent for Alaska in 1885. During the next 20 years he labored to bring schools to all parts of the region. Jackson's goal was to protect young Natives within a framework of law and, through education, prepare them to cope with modern times. His efforts were welcomed by some Natives and they were generally consistent with mainstream non-Native assumptions of the day. Yet many critics now think that mission schools, by discouraging the use of indigenous languages and a paternalistic emphasis on assimilation, hastened an unhealthy decline of Native traditions and undermined the self-confident ability of some children to deal with changing times.

The Organic Act was an improvement over military government, but it had its flaws. Liquor prohibition, unenforceable from a practical standpoint over such a large territory, was retained at Jackson's adamant insistence. Without prohibition, Jackson feared, Natives would be completely unprotected from the influence of rum. Rum in itself was a scourge to Natives, and much bootlegged liquor was nothing but lethal rotgut. Total prohibition, however, was counterproductive. Yet Jackson, with his Washington connections, always prevailed against the anti-prohibition forces until the gold rush. Then, awash with alcohol, Alaska at last introduced a liquor licensing system in 1899.

John Muir and Glacier Bay

John Muir

John Muir, the famous naturalist, conservationist, and Sierra Club founder, played a crucial role in publicizing Alaska's natural wonders to the outside world. Born in Scotland in 1838, Muir came to America as a boy of 11 and moved to California in 1868. A prodigious walker with a mystical regard for nature, Muir trekked the High Sierra and, like Wordsworth, Emerson, and Thoreau, described his travels with an evocative flair. To Muir, nature was a rustic trail to the sublime—the steeper, the better.

An amateur scientist as well as a romantic, Muir sought in his wanderings to vindicate the then-controversial idea that glaciers once covered much of the northern hemisphere. He believed that glaciers, not rivers, carved some of the earth's most spectacular geological features such as his beloved Yosemite Valley. This fascination with glaciers drew Muir northward for the first time in 1879.

With four Tlingit paddlers and the Presbyterian missionary S. Hall Young, Muir set out from Wrangell by canoe on October 14, 1879. From prospectors he had heard of wonderful glaciers around the Lynn Canal, and one of his Native companions, Sitka Charley, remembered hunting for seals with his father in a "large bay full of ice." Winter was near but, as Muir laconically recalled in *Travels in Alaska*, "I was familiar with storms and enjoyed them."

In light of the late season, the Tlingit were none too sure of the adventure's wisdom, but Reverend Young welcomed the chance to preach to villagers along the way. At length the party arrived at Icy Strait, encountering by luck a group of Hoonah sealers who, after initial skepticism, agreed to guide them into the inlet now famous as Glacier Bay. The explorer Vancouver passed by it in 1794 but had not remarked on the area since the fjord was then entirely choked with ice. But in the years since, ice in the bay had receded at an astounding rate, so that Muir found a complex of flooded canyons reaching far back into the towering Fairweather Range.

Massive tidewater glaciers loomed at the head of many inlets, shedding enormous chunks of ice into the sea. Muir was overwhelmed. Clambering 1,500 feet above the party's first, mist-enshrouded campsite, Muir saw through the parted clouds "a solitude of ice and snow and newborn rocks, dim, dreary, mysterious." Later, inspecting a glacier face at close range, he marveled at the spectrum of icy blues, from "pale, shimmering, limpid tones in the crevasses and hollows, to the most startling, chilling, almost shrieking vitriol blue on the plain mural spaces from which bergs had just been discharged."

Muir's reports to the San Francisco press of his 800-mile canoe trip helped inaugurate Alaska tourism. Cruises to the bay began in 1883, and by 1890 some 25,000 sightseers had traveled the upper Inside Passage.

With 18 tidewater glaciers, the most in a single bay anywhere, Glacier Bay remains a magnet for southeastern Alaska tourists, who also flock to see the bay's abundant harbor seals and humpback whales. Part of the national park system since 1925, the bay affords modern visitors, just as it did Muir over a century ago, the chance to re-enter the Ice Age.

Gold Fever Before the Klondike Strike

The Treadwell Mine near Juneau, about 1886.

Gold fever ran at a high pitch in the wake of strikes in California in 1848 and in British Columbia's Fraser River, Stikine, and Cassiar country in the 1850s, 1860s, and 1870s. Not surprisingly, boosters of the 1867 purchase of Alaska extolled the region's potential mineral wealth. In fact, the Russian mining engineer Peter Doroshin discovered small deposits of gold on Alaska's Kenai Peninsula as early as 1850. But the Russian-American Company was mainly interested in the "soft gold" of sea otter fur.

While southeastern Alaska's Skagway and the Canadian Yukon's Klondike region may first come to mind when thinking about the gold rush era, gold in the Far North is not the story of one strike alone.

A string of strikes began shortly after 1867 when federal soldiers, prospecting in their spare time, made modest finds around Sitka. The first major strike, by the French-Canadian Joe Juneau and his partner Richard Harris, came in 1880 at Gold Creek—the site of present-day Juneau. The two men had been outfitted by a

German-immigrant mining engineer named George Pilz and were led to the site at Quartz Gulch by Chief Kowee of the Auk Tlingit clan.

In a decade, the little town blossomed to a population of 1,200, and by the turn of the century, mines in the vicinity—the Silver Bow, the Alaska-Juneau, the Alaska-Gastineau, and the Treadwell—had produced over $17 million in gold. (Symbolizing gold's commercial triumph over furs, Juneau would replace Sitka as Alaska's capital in 1906.)

With 880 stamps—rock pulverizers that weighed 900 pounds apiece—the hard-rock Treadwell Mill on Douglas Island, directly across from town, was one of the world's largest quartz-crushing operations. Native American and East European laborers worked within for the then-lofty wage of $2.50 a day. A visitor in the early 1890s reported that the acidic smoke from a Treadwell plant had destroyed vegetation "for a mile up and down the island's edge." The mill used the latest mining technology to recover the tiniest mineral traces from the region's low-grade ore. The end result—two sizes of gold bricks worth either $15,000 or $18,000—were shipped monthly to the U.S. mint in San Francisco.

Forty-Mile River in 1886 was the first important gold find in the Interior, located just inside Alaska on the Yukon border. A camp was established at Forty-Mile in the Yukon, not far from present-day Dawson. Another important strike came at Circle City in 1893 (so named because its founders mistakenly believed it was north of the Arctic Circle). The site—which soon boasted a population of 1,000 men and 40 women, most of them dance-hall girls with names like "Black Kitty" and "Ella the Glacier"—was located on a Yukon River tributary, about 240 miles downriver from Forty-Mile. To serve the burgeoning area, steamboat traffic began to move up the Yukon all the way from St. Michael, more than 1,000 miles away on the Bering Sea. The penetration of the vast northern Interior had begun.

THE KLONDIKE STAMPEDE

Skagway, Alaska. May 20, 1898.

The North's most famous bonanza came with the 1896 discovery of rich placer deposits on Rabbit Creek, a tributary of the Klondike River in the Canadian Yukon. The find by George Washington Carmack and his Indian partners, Skookum Jim and Tagish Charlie, led to the founding of Dawson City.

In the two years after the find, 40,000 people arrived in the valley. Another 60,000 set out for the Klondike, but turned back, fell ill, or stopped along the way. The newcomers hailed from all corners of the earth. Most, however, were Americans, and most were greenhorns ("cheechakos" in the Chinook trading jargon). The nation's economy had been in the doldrums, and some fortune seekers were unemployed vagabonds. But all sorts of men and women, prosperous and desperate alike, joined the mad rush. Few had any notion of the hardships required to reach the gold fields.

Most stampeders came by steamship from Seattle, up the Inside Passage to the new Alaska ports of Dyea or nearby Skagway. Then, laden with a year's provisions as required by the Canadian Mounted Police—a half-ton burden—they trekked the 40 miles over White or Chilkoot pass. At Dead Horse Gulch, 17.5 miles up the White Pass trail, thousands of exhausted and abused pack animals met their end in the frenzied rush.

Martha Purdy of Chicago, later Martha Black, a prominent Dawson businesswoman and Canadian Member of Parliament, climbed in the latest outing costume: high leather boots with elk hide soles, a heavy corduroy skirt of "shockingly immodest length" (it showed her ankles), a high buckram collar, "tight heavily boned corsets," and "a pair of voluminous brown silk bloomers" that she "had to hitch up with every step."

Out of Dyea, stampeders encountered the Chilkoot Trail's most notorious stretch—the Golden Stairs, a 30-degree grade just below the summit where, in winter, steps were carved into the ice to ease the ascent. Working in two-man relays, a team of stampeders might require 20 or more one-hour trips to haul their combined 2,000 pounds of goods to the top. Inevitably, disasters struck: an April 1898 avalanche buried 63 people.

When the narrow-gauge White Pass & Yukon Route railroad was completed in July 1900, Skagway's rival, Dyea, faded into a ghost town as the Skagway-to-White-Pass tracks replaced both routes to the Klondike. Construction gangs on the two-year rail project worked in winter temperatures of –60 degrees Fahrenheit. From sea level at Skagway, the track climbed 2,865 feet in 20 switchback miles to the White Pass summit on the Canadian border.

Once in Canada, at Lindemann or Bennett lakes, the stampeders built boats and floated 550 miles by river to Dawson. After the ice broke in May 1898, 7,000 boats headed downriver in a single week. Today's hikers can see firsthand the gold rush's rusty remnants by retracing the Chilkoot Trail, now managed by the U.S. and Canadian park services.

Despite the hardships, tens of thousands completed the journey, and helped extract more than $300 million in Klondike gold. Only a few sourdoughs actually struck it rich. Even fewer managed to hang on to their riches. Still, many of the disappointed fanned out across Alaska and helped to find or exploit new discoveries.

Stirring Days in Skagway

Soapy Smith at the bar of his Skagway saloon, 1898.

Villains and hucksters abounded in the gold-rush boom towns of Skagway and neighboring Dyea in the summer of 1898. Even Skagway's birth was illegitimate. Eleven years earlier, 65-year-old Captain Billy Moore had staked a claim to 160 acres on the Skagway River at the north end of the Lynn Canal. When the first stampeders arrived at the site aboard the mail steamer *Queen* in July 1897, their leaders simply jumped Moore's claim and laid out a town on their own.

At the height of the rush, boats from the south arrived almost daily, packed with potential prey for shady dealers. Most notorious of the Skagway con men was the Georgia-born Jefferson Randolph ("Soapy") Smith. He allegedly earned his nickname in Colorado and Nevada mining towns selling bars of soap wrapped in counterfeit $20 bills.

Martha Purdy, a stampeder who first saw him as her steamer *Utopia* approached the Skagway waterfront, described him as "a fine figure of a man with heavy flowing black mustaches, mounted on a white horse." Skagway was a roaring camp and Smith for a time became its leading citizen—in the wharf district, that is, where greenhorns infected by what Alaska governor John G. Brady called "klondicitis" stepped off the boats.

Soapy, who owned a Skagway drinking and gambling den called Jeff's Place, had a Barnumesque talent for inventing ingenious scams. His agents roamed the Seattle docks, advising stampeders to visit Soapy's saloon for information once they arrived in the north. Those who fell for this advice became easy targets for his gang's fraudulent schemes. He ran a telegraph office where for $5 newcomers might wire relatives in the south that they had safely arrived in Skagway. They didn't know that telegraph lines had yet to reach the town, but somehow there was always a prompt and comforting response from their families.

Smith also posed as a patriot. He recruited groups of discouraged stampeders to travel to Cuba to fight in the Spanish American War. While volunteers were undressed at his "recruiting station" to undergo the necessary "medical examination," members of Smith's gang rifled their clothes for money and valuables.

Smith's schemes came to an abrupt and violent end in July 1898, after members of his gang lured a sourdough named Stewart into Jeff's Place, clubbed him, and stole his poke of gold worth $2,700. In response, business leaders and the city surveyor, Frank Reid, formed a vigilante group to eliminate the gang.

Reid himself had a somewhat checkered past. Several years earlier he had been acquitted on grounds of self-defense for killing a man in Oregon, though the man was reportedly unarmed. After Billy Moore's claim had been jumped, it was Reid who surveyed the new town site.

On the night of July 8, a few days after Soapy had led the Independence Day parade, Reid confronted Smith on the city dock. Shots were exchanged. Both men died, Smith immediately and Reid several days later. Soapy's gang was rounded up and sent south to Seattle. Both Smith and Reid were buried nearby.

Still savoring its gold-rush heritage, Skagway ironically now honors Smith each July with participants gathering in town to toast Soapy's name.

New Eldorados:
Nome and Fairbanks

The beach and tent city at Nome, 1900. Photo by E.A. Hegg.

As miners first drawn north by the Klondike strike fanned across Alaska, it didn't take long to hit gold again. Three Scandinavian prospectors struck pay dirt at Cape Nome in late 1898.

The following July, gold was found nearby mixed in the sand along the Bering Sea. Wild stories spread that the sea floor was covered with gold, and by the summer of 1900, 20,000 people crowded a tent city on the beach. The Nome gold fields the next year yielded the biggest nugget ever found in Alaska: seven-by-four-by-two inches weighing 107 ounces, 2 pennyweight.

Unlike Dawson in the Yukon, where Canada's Mounties kept order, early Nome was lawless. Every miner was armed, and claim jumping was common. A federal judge, Arthur H. Noyes, was appointed in 1900 to bring order to chaos. Noyes ordered all disputed claims placed in receivership, then appointed Alexander McKenzie (a former North Dakota sheriff, political boss, and Washington lobbyist) as trustee. McKenzie reopened the mines, then split the take with the corrupt Noyes. The pair became rich overnight.

Eventually a delegation of defrauded miners persuaded a higher San Francisco court to overturn Noyes' decision. McKenzie—who hatched the entire scheme—was taken to San Francisco, tried, and sentenced to a one-year prison term. President William McKinley later reduced his sentence to three months due to McKenzie's "poor health." Several months later, Noyes was stripped of his office, fined

$1,000, and the respected Judge James Wickersham was brought in to clean up the town.

The next great gold strike came in 1902 in the heart of Alaska. Felix Pedro, an Italian immigrant, found gold in the hills of the Tanana Valley. A trading post sprang up where the Chena River met the Tanana. Its boosters named it Fairbanks, after Indiana Senator Charles Fairbanks, who later became Teddy Roosevelt's vice-president.

Like Nome, early Fairbanks was a roaring camp. In 1904, 33 saloons flourished in a four-block stretch of First Avenue. Reports of the wealth spread to Dawson, where Chee-chaco Lil, a famous madam, decided to relocate to the new town. Lil's debut in Fairbanks signaled the beginning of a prostitutes' stampede rivaling that of the miners. But it wasn't long before the miner's camp took on the trappings of a proper town.

Fairbanks was largely settled not by greenhorns but by veteran miners from the Yukon or Nome who often brought wives and children with them. The first school opened in 1904, and Fairbanks was soon calling itself the world's largest log town.

Fairbanks went up in flames on May 22, 1906, when a great fire destroyed much of the log settlement. But the town's rough-and-ready optimism remained undiminished. A day after the blaze the owner of one burned-out saloon set up shop outside, alongside a banner reading "fresh bar, fresh air and good treatment."

The community's residents managed to convince authorities that a rail line should be built inland from the southcentral coast. After much delay, the 400-mile Alaska Railroad was begun in 1915 at Seward on the Gulf of Alaska, running past what became Anchorage and north through the Alaska Range. To mark the project's completion, in 1923 President Warren Harding drove in the golden spike at Nenana, 50 miles west of Fairbanks.

THE YUKON:
HIGHWAY TO THE INTERIOR

 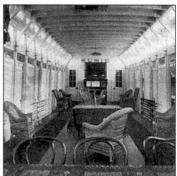

Yukon sternwheeler Sarah *(left) and social hall of the* Susie.

From its headwaters near the Chilkoot Pass in northern British Columbia, the Yukon River flows in a grand westerly arc to the Bering Sea. Its 2,000-mile course is longer than the Colorado, the Columbia, or the Rio Grande. The river drains 330,000 square miles, and its tributaries include the Klondike, the Porcupine, the Tanana, and the Koyukuk. Small wonder that the Athabascan word "yukonna" means "great river."

For much of its length, the river travels through flat country. Its channels and banks shift constantly, aided by annual floods caused by ice jams during spring break up. Between June and September shallow-draft boats can navigate the treacherous river for virtually its entire length, from its mouth on Norton Sound to its birthplace near Canada's Lake Bennett.

Since prehistory, the Yukon's brown ribbon has undulated across Alaska's Interior. During the last Ice Age, 10,000 years ago, the Yukon's arid valley remained glacier free. For some of Alaska's early visitors, nomadic hunters from Asia, it became a gateway to the rest of North America. Later, Eskimos and Athabascans used it as a trade route. Russian American and Hudson's Bay fur traders extended their operations up the Yukon to the Interior by canoe and keelboat in the 1830s and 1840s.

In 1869 Parrott & Company inaugurated an 80-year chapter in

Alaska's history by launching the river's first sternwheel steamboat, a 50-foot packet fittingly named the *Yukon*. It and its small sister vessels, the *New Racket* and the *St. Michael*, carried trade goods each summer to company posts in the Interior and sped downriver with furs just before freeze-up.

The gold rushes of the 1890s signaled the classic age of the Yukon riverboat, as the Alaska Commercial Company and its competitors vied for the dollars of stampeders and outfitters in boom towns like Dawson, Nome, and Fairbanks.

Powerful, 200-foot-long sternwheelers like the *Sarah*, the *Susie*, and the *Hannah* were built with double decks, dual smokestacks, ornate dining rooms, and carpeted saloons. The *Susie*, recalled Judge James Wickersham, "made a strange but beautiful spectacle as she sped down-stream in the arctic twilight . . . like a fairy palace floating noiselessly through the dark green forests."

Aided by river-wise Athabascan pilots, captains like James T. Gray—known to his crew as the "Master of Impressive Profanity"— threaded these flat-bottomed giants and their companion barges through the river's innumerable snags and bars. To move cargo up the Yukon's shallower tributaries, Gray designed the *Koyukuk*, which was 120 feet long with a draft of only 9½ inches. Many a failed sourdough found work along the river cutting the thousands of cords of wood consumed by the voracious river queens.

Completion of the Alaska Railroad in 1923 and the later advent of cargo aircraft spelled the end of Alaska's sternwheeler age. One last, great paddlewheeler was built in 1930—the *Nenana*—but after World War II she had the river to herself and was finally retired in the 1950s. Yet the memory of the last frontier's riverboat era remained vivid for Alaska pioneers. "So long as we heard the chuff and whoosh of that wheel," recalled writer Margaret Murie, "we knew all was fine, and I know, to this day, of no more soothing, competent, all-is-well sound."

Frontier Tourism:
Alaska with Baedeker

Early tourists at the Muir Glacier, Glacier Bay, 1885.

Klondike gold garnered world attention and enticed not only miners, but waves of tourists, to the Far North. Even before the Klondike strike, the travel industry was a going concern—at least in southeastern Alaska. In 1882, General Nelson Miles, the local Army commandant, led a travel group aboard the steamer *Dakota* up the Inside Passage. A year later, Captain James C. Carrol took visitors on the *Idaho* into Glacier Bay. Soon steamship companies arranged to have their tickets sold by major rail lines in New York and Montreal, enabling travelers to end their transcontinental excursion with an Alaska cruise. During the summer of 1890 alone, 5,000 visitors sailed the Inside Passage.

When rising affluence in Europe and America sparked early tourism, the raspberry-red travel guides published by the German firm of Karl Baedeker were synonymous with travel. No knowledgeable tourist left home without his or her "Baedeker." The inclusion of several pages on Alaska in Baedeker's 1904 handbook for the United States was proof that Alaska had arrived as an international tourist destination.

The Pacific Coast Steamship Company of San Francisco, highly recommended by Baedeker, ruled early Alaska tourism. The company's steamer, the *Spokane*, sailed from Tacoma six times each summer for the 11-day round trip to Skagway and Glacier Bay. Fares ranged from $100 for basic accommodations to $250 for one's own "large deck state-room." This was considered a travel bargain for, while the *Spokane* fell short of ocean liner luxury, it was quite comfortable. Veterans of European travel were assured the journey involved no more danger than cruising Norway's fjords. Along the Inside Passage, Baedeker editors promised that passengers would witness "the indescribably beautiful effects of the late sunsets (9–10 P.M.)."

Pioneer travelers were fascinated by Native life. The Haida village of Old Kasaan near Ketchikan, with its mysterious old totem poles, became an occasional port of call. Enterprising Natives conducted a lively trade in craft items. At Wrangell, visitors bought engraved silver bracelets, carved horn and wooden spoons, woven baskets, carved halibut hooks, painted canoe paddles, and even shamans' carved raven rattles.

Juneau and Skagway shops offered famous Chilkat blankets made from mountain-goat hair and colored with Native dyes. Baedeker warned collectors, however, that authentic pieces, "worth $60–100, are now rare, and most of those offered for sale are made of [sheep's] wool and stained with aniline dyes."

At Skagway, the *Spokane* docked long enough for passengers to take an adventuresome excursion to White Pass on the newly completed narrow-gauge railroad. At the summit, Baedeker suggested, "good echoes may be wakened off the glaciers."

Then, as now, Glacier Bay was the high point. The spectacular Muir Glacier, Baedeker declared, cast even "the large ice fields of Switzerland entirely into the shade." In August, Baedeker reported, "200,000,000 cubic feet of ice fall into the inlet daily."

In Alaska, the guidebook assured readers, one would encounter scenery "of the most grand and unique character, such as, probably, cannot be seen elsewhere at so little cost and with so little toil or adventure."

The Excelsior departs San Francisco—the first ship to Alaska after news of the Klondike strike, July 28, 1897.

ALASKA IN THE TWENTIETH CENTURY: FROM TERRITORY TO STATEHOOD

AFTER '98

Stampeders and their supplies at Dyea, about 1898.

It's difficult to exaggerate the impact of the gold rush on Alaska's future. The Russians built an Alaskan empire, but their numbers were few. Other early explorers came and went, leaving little trace of their passage. But gold fever sent thousands of outsiders deep into the heart of the territory. Between 1890 and 1900, the region's year-round population doubled—from about 30,000 to over 60,000.

Other major changes were close behind. The first roads and railways were built, and Congress extended to Alaska a limited version of the Homestead Act: anyone who pledged to live and work on the land could have 80 acres for free. Shortly after the turn of the century Washington also sent teams of agronomists to study the farming potential of certain areas, such as the Matanuska Valley north of Cook Inlet and the Tanana Valley in the Interior near the new settlement of Fairbanks. The discovery of gold in the Far North captured the attention of the American public, and the world. For the first time the government was actually encouraging permanent settlement in the region. The sudden population growth, publicity, and outside investment fueled far-reaching political changes as well.

In 1906 Alaskans were allowed to send a nonvoting delegate to Washington, D.C., to sit in the U.S. House of Representatives. At last, Alaska had a voice in the nation's capital. Most memorable of the early Alaska delegates was the widely respected Judge James Wickersham, first elected in 1908. While he had no vote, the energetic Wickersham was a tireless lobbyist for the region and drafted the first bill for Alaska statehood in 1916.

The statehood bill went nowhere; critics scoffed at Alaska's remoteness, the alleged naiveté or outright political indifference of its white and Native residents, and its sheer lack of population to provide a tax base for local government operations. However, one of Wickersham's legislative projects, the "Home Rule" act of 1912, did win territorial status for Alaska. Under the law, Alaskans were finally allowed to elect a territorial legislature. Women as well as men received the right to vote—well before the Nineteenth Amendment of 1920 granted that power to women nationwide.

But the new law had its limits. Under its terms Alaska's governor, as in the past, was a presidential appointee. Alaska remained an effective colony of the Lower 48, since the area's natural wealth remained under federal jurisdiction, which often favored politically powerful commercial interests in Seattle, San Francisco, and New York. Favoritism and the laxity of federal controls and enforcement would, in the future, threaten even the Great Land's seemingly limitless natural abundance. Such entanglement of economic and environmental issues was to become a major theme of Alaska's history in the next century.

Despite the law's limitations, many Alaskans were proud of the limited voice they had attained in their own affairs. To a few dreamers it seemed possible that Alaska might someday become a state.

Pioneer Judge:
James W. Wickersham

Wickersham campaign flyer, 1914.

Despite early Alaska's many legendary villains and plunderers, not all the northern frontier's colorful characters were scoundrels. One of the most interesting—and historically important—figures was Judge James W. Wickersham, Alaska's preeminent political personality during the early 1900s.

Wickersham, born in Illinois in 1857, came to Alaska in 1900 as federal judge for the newly created Third Judicial Division—aboard the same steamer, ironically, as the corrupt Judge Noyes he would one day replace. A hardy six feet tall, "Wick" was a man of many talents: jurist, outdoorsman and adventurer, politician, and writer. His first, daunting task was to introduce jurisprudence to the third district, 300,000 square miles of wilderness sprawling from the Arctic Slope in the north to the Aleutians in the southwest—about half of Alaska's territory.

Before his arrival, the "miner's code" prevailed—an earthy mode of democratic justice whereby camp residents gathered whenever a dispute arose and resolved the issue by majority vote. Punishments were equally rough-hewn: hanging for murder, banishment or flogging for lesser crimes.

The energetic judge relished the challenge. Establishing his first court in the Yukon River settlement of Eagle, he summoned prostitutes and card sharks before the bench. They could ply their respective trades, he told them, but only if they paid a periodic fine "in vindication of the laws and as an aid to the fund to maintain the police."

Wickersham carried justice to other outposts, such as Circle and Rampart, via sternwheeler in summer and dogsled in winter. He routinely presided over 12-hour hearings until all disputes were successfully resolved. By cleaning up a 1901 scandal in Nome involving a crooked former sheriff and a corrupt judge, Wickersham confirmed his growing reputation for honest, calm efficiency, and even-handed fairness. From Nome the judge moved his court to Fairbanks. From there in 1903, he led the first unsuccessful attempt to scale Mount McKinley (now called Denali)—between court sessions.

Renowned for his integrity on the bench, when it came to campaigning for office Wickersham was a born politician, a riveting speaker who—in the words of an unfriendly editor—assailed his opponents with whatever was handy: "blades, war clubs/truth/lies." Known for his populist crusades against bureaucratic corruption and big business, he was elected as Alaska's nonvoting congressional delegate in 1908. Wickersham effectively served as the region's voice in Washington, D.C., from 1909 to 1921, and again from 1931 to 1933. His achievements included gaining territorial status for Alaska in 1912, and four years later introducing the first bill for Alaska statehood. Wick also won congressional approval for the Alaska Railroad from Seward to Fairbanks in 1914, the establishment of Mount McKinley (now Denali) National Park in 1917, and—in the same year—the creation of the Agricultural College and School of Mines in Fairbanks (now the University of Alaska).

In his later years, prior to his death in 1939, Judge Wickersham lived in Juneau. His house on Chicken Ridge is now a museum and Alaska state historic site open to the public.

A Young Girl's Fairbanks

Residential street in Fairbanks, early 1900s.

Margaret Murie was a girl of nine in 1911 when she traveled by steamer with her mother from Seattle to Dawson, then by sternwheeler down the Yukon River to join her stepfather, an assistant U.S. attorney in Fairbanks. As Murie reports in her Alaskan memoir, *Two in the Far North*, a small girl "can see and hear a lot."

Through keen observation and conversations with her elders, she soon learned the inner workings of the log boomtown that became her childhood home. (She would later become the University of Alaska's first woman graduate, wife and field partner of Alaska biologist, Olaus Murie, and a celebrated environmental writer.) In these frontier camps, where winters tried the soul, people had a mission—to seize the day and become rich. "All was costly, everything was done on a lavish scale," she writes. "The finest things that could be hauled into this country from Outside were none too good for these pioneers . . . If all might be lost in a season in the diggings, then they would have the best while they could."

There were modern conveniences for Margaret's mother: electricity to heat the new iron, and a telephone. In a storeroom adjoining the house, called the cache, ample supplies of frozen moose, caribou, and fish were laid in for the winter. Warmed by cords of split spruce that fired the stove, the family's cabin, like the town, was a "little bastion against the 50-below-zero world outside."

Fairbanks, Margaret discovered, held two towns in one. "The town you could talk about" was occupied by merchants, attorneys, bankers—a proper society of latecomers who served the more reputable needs of the town's founders, the miners. Twenty-three saloons—"as though they were the first things the early settlers thought of"— lined Front Street, the town's outer face along the banks of Chena Slough. At the very center stood "the Row," a red-light district of one-room huts stretching for three blocks along Fourth.

By the time Margaret arrived, a fence stood at each end to conceal the quarter's activities, although not very successfully. The good neighborhood, after all, began on Fifth, immediately behind the Row. And just a block and a half away stood the courthouse from where Margaret's father and three colleagues enforced "virtue and observance of the law throughout the Fourth Judicial Division... an area of 220,000 square miles!"

Despite its social divisions the town was a community. Fundraisers accepted donations from ladies of the evening, and charity was extended if an ever-dreaded fire destroyed a cabin in the Row. "There was a good deal of live-and-let-live... We were all far away from the rest of the world; we had to depend on one another."

Children, a rarity in a settlement of predominantly single men, were a pampered elite. "We lived in an atmosphere of tolerance and love... Every family... had some miner or trapper friend who became more or less a member—who came in from the creeks for special days, who was there for Thanksgiving and Christmas. And what Santa Clauses they were!"

KING COPPER

The Kennecott Mine, early 1900s.

Gold was not the only mineral to fire men's imaginations in Alaska. The Tlingit and other Northwest Coast Indians revered above all symbols of rank and wealth so-called "coppers" (tinnehs), large, flat sheets of beaten copper. The most dramatic way for a potlatch host to demonstrate his wealth was to break a copper or throw it into the sea.

White wealth seekers were driven mainly by dreams of gold but some were excited by visions of copper as well. As the 1880s drew to a close, stories of a mountain of copper, somewhere in the Wrangell–St. Elias Range, spread among Alaska sourdoughs. But the metal's exact source long remained a secret, aided by the unfriendly reputation of local Athabascan Indians. One early trader was killed in 1884 when he became too inquisitive about the rumored lode.

In late summer 1900, a team of adventurous prospectors operating 200 miles north of the Gulf of Alaska along the Chitina River (a tributary of the Copper River) stumbled upon a massive cliff of green rock. When they analyzed samples, they discovered the ore was 70 percent copper and included some silver and gold as well. They had uncovered one of the earth's richest copper reserves.

The men staked a mile-long claim, then foolishly sold it to a mining engineer named Stephen Birch, who founded the Alaska

Copper and Coal Company to work the find. But the region was so remote, and the terrain so difficult, that Birch could not effectively work the mine. In 1908 the steel magnate J.P. Morgan and the Guggenheim brothers of New York joined to buy out Birch and form the "Alaska Syndicate" to exploit the site. Through their Kennecott Copper Company, the Guggenheims and Morgan cornered copper production, for they alone had the financial clout to get the job done in the rugged country.

To accomplish the task, they took five years to build a $23 million company railway to reach from the port of Cordova to the mines 200 miles upriver. Mining began in 1911, and soon the overall value of copper production in Alaska actually exceeded that of gold: by 1916 Alaska yielded over $29 million in copper compared to $19 million in gold. Before the mine closed in 1938 it produced 1 billion tons of copper and 9.7 million ounces of silver worth a combined $300 million—a dollar sum practically equal to that produced by gold.

Of course, little of the wealth remained in Alaska itself. From copper the Syndicate branched into salmon canning, gold mining, and transportation, with its Alaska Steamship Company. The Syndicate, popularly known as "the Guggs," quickly grew into the most powerful of the outside interests that many permanent Alaska residents and newspaper editorial writers resented so much. Pioneer politician James Wickersham built his colorful career on denunciations of the New York Syndicate.

Today all that remains of the Kennecott operation are some ramshackle, rusty-roofed sheds and a few hamlets like McCarthy. The wild character of the Kennecott country is preserved by America's largest parkland, Wrangell–St. Elias National Park, created in 1980 within boundaries six times larger than Yellowstone's. The town of Cordova survives as a fishing port; Copper River king and sockeye salmon, world renowned for their rich flesh and exceptionally high oil content, have replaced minerals as the area's major resource.

Anchorage and the Iron Horse

The birth of Anchorage, 1915.

The late 1800s were the heyday of empire-building railroad barons and, after the gold rush, Alaskan railway schemes abounded with names like the Tanana Valley Railroad, the Wild Goose Railway, and the 15-mile Yakutat and Southern Line, which hauled salmon between Situk and Lost River and Yakutat. Only two of the early projects lasted long: the narrow-gauge White Pass and Yukon Route, built with British money from Skagway over Canada's Coast Mountains to the Klondike gold fields, and the Guggenheim brothers' Copper River and Northwestern Railroad, from Cordova on Prince William Sound to their copper mines upstream on the Chitina River.

A third line, the Alaska Central, running north from Seward on the Kenai Peninsula, was promoted in 1903 to carry coal from the Matanuska Valley. Fifty miles of track were laid, but despite rosy predictions by the line's Seattle backers, the company went bankrupt by 1908.

Yet Alaska boosters yearned for a railroad into the Interior, especially after the Fairbanks gold strike of 1902. Federal officials eventually agreed, and in 1914 surveyors traveled north to study various routes. In the following year, President Woodrow Wilson ruled in favor of extending the existing Alaska Central track. His decision launched America's only government railway, the 470-mile Alaska Railroad from Seward on the Gulf of Alaska to Fairbanks in Alaska's heart.

In April 1915 a wilderness construction camp was established at Knik Anchorage on Cook Inlet. Overnight, a tent city of 2,000 people sprang up, spawning Anchorage. Soon a proper townsite was surveyed on nearby clay bluffs overlooking Ship Creek, and in July lots were auctioned to the public. Officials hoped to avoid the rowdy examples of mining towns like Skagway and Nome, and so lots were sold only if they were not "used for the purpose of manufacturing, selling, or otherwise disposing of intoxicating liquors as a beverage, or for gambling, prostitution, or any unlawful purpose."

No community enjoyed an easier birth or a more pampered childhood. Utilities, fire protection, a hospital, schools, and city management were all initially supplied by the federal government. With the railroad as its economic base, Anchorage became the region's premier distribution and financial center. Today nearly 300,000 people live there—close to half of Alaska's population.

As for the railroad itself, following delays caused by World War I, it was finished for a total of $65 million in 1923. President Warren Harding came to Nenana, 50 miles southwest of Fairbanks, to drive the golden spike.

After some initial rough years marred by bad management and labor disputes, the line turned a profit under the direction of Otto Ohlson, the general manager from 1928 to 1946. In the Cold War era, the Alaska line's nearness to Russia gave it strategic value for the United States, and it was practically rebuilt in the late 1940s. The 1964 earthquake, however, caused $27 million in damage to the line, and it gradually lost ground to other forms of transport.

But bolstered by Alaska's booming travel industry, the railroad has become a major attraction for tourists bound for Denali National Park.

BUSH PILOTS

Carl Ben Eielson (left), 1920s, and Harold Gillam, about 1930.

America's love affair with the automobile is legendary. Since the 1920s, Alaska—with its unbridged waters, impassable mountains, and roadless tundra—has been in love with the airplane. The romance springs from necessity as well as infatuation. Travel in the Far North demands planes. By the late 1900s, one in forty-five Alaska residents held a pilot's license—six times the national average.

The end of World War I signaled takeoff for Alaska commercial aviation. Ten thousand newly minted flyers were demobilized, and thousands of military "airships" were dumped on the surplus market. In the 1920s, when Midwestern barnstormers captured the nation's imagination, a handful of aerial adventurers introduced Alaska to aviation.

In 1922, Roy Jones made the first flight up the Inside Passage from Seattle to Ketchikan, landing in the Tongass Narrows where floatplanes now swarm like mosquitoes. Air travel transformed the Alaskan bush. Where sternwheeler and sled dog had been king, roaring engines now broke the solitude and blazed aerial trails. River and overland delivery of mail and cargo soon became a thing of the past.

The North's bracing climate presented special challenges. Engines and oil had to be kept warm in −50 degree weather, spare propellers were lashed to fuselages, and crashes were part of a flyer's job description. Lacking instruments or reliable maps, aviators followed rivers, railroads, and pack trails—when they were visible. Pilots doubled as wonder-working mechanics or developed strong legs hiking out from crack-ups in the bush.

The romance of Arctic flight captured world notice in 1928, when pilots Carl Ben Eielson and Australian-born George Hubert Wilkins flew from Barrow to Spitsbergen, Norway—the first polar flight from America to Europe. Eielson, who came to Fairbanks in 1922, inaugurated Alaska mail runs and commercial air service in the Interior. In 1929 he tried to salvage $1 million in furs from the ice-bound ship *Nanuk* off the Siberian coast. His disappearance set off a much publicized search. Two months later, Joe Crosson and Harold Gillam, two other famous pilots, found the downed plane and the frozen bodies of Eielson and his mechanic.

Crosson made history by becoming the first pilot to land on a glacier. In April of 1932, he flew three scientists, plus several hundred pounds of gear, to the 6,000-foot level of Denali's Muldrow Glacier. Gillam exemplified the classic bush pilot's strong stomach, charmed life, and fatalistic ethos. While learning to fly he survived a crash that killed his own instructor. He walked away from six crashes in 1931 alone. In 1943 his luck ran out when his Lockheed Electra, carrying five passengers, went down in fog near Ketchikan.

The most influential of the Alaska pioneer flyers, in the long run, were the Wien brothers of Minnesota: Noel, Ralph, Fritz, and Sig. Noel came to Alaska in 1924 and established Wien Airways (eventually Wien Air Alaska), which made Fairbanks the hub of Alaskan aviation. Each time he went south he returned with a brother to help manage and build the company. Himself a barnstorming ace, Noel displayed slightly more caution than others in the flying fraternity. His motto: "Take 'em out and bring 'em back."

The "Thousand-Mile War": The Aleutian Campaign of World War II

Aleutian Skies, World War II.

Alaska's isolation sheltered the region from World War I, but technical progress and Japanese aggression created a new setting in World War II—a fact at first not fully appreciated by America's leaders. The Aleutian Islands were a likely Japanese target; after all, San Francisco is more than 1,000 miles closer to Tokyo via the Aleutian Islands than it is through Honolulu. Still, authorities did little to create defenses in the Aleutians aside from a small base at Dutch Harbor in 1940. Like Hawaii, Alaska was unprepared for its day of infamy.

A 1942 Japanese attack on Alaska was designed to divert American air and naval strength northward during a simultaneous effort at destroying America's fleet in the central Pacific. On June 3, 1942, a Japanese fleet including two aircraft carriers and two heavy cruisers launched a raid on Dutch Harbor. The invaders lost the element of surprise, however: on the previous day a patrol plane had spotted the fleet through a break in the clouds, and American gunners repelled the attack. Nor did the operation succeed in its diversionary aim; the central Pacific's Battle of Midway marked a defeat for Japan and became a turning point in the war.

Yet Japan decided to remain in the Aleutians, hoping that its positions there might forestall a possible American invasion of Japan itself. On June 7, 1942, 1,200 Japanese troops landed on the sparsely populated and undefended islands of Attu and Kiska, where they built an air base, bunkers, and anti-aircraft emplacements. Japanese offensive operations essentially ended after late July 1942, and the war became a Japanese struggle to maintain its precarious hold in the face of relentless American air attacks. The gray, blustery climate proved an ally—more American aircraft were lost to violent gales and low visibility than to Japanese fire. The campaign's climax began on May 11, 1943, when 11,000 American troops landed on Attu. Colonel Yasuyo Yamasaki defended the island with 2,600 troops. After 18 days, only 800 combat-capable Japanese remained. Yamasaki ordered all the disabled troops to kill themselves. Those incapable of suicide were given lethal doses of morphine. The remaining men attacked early on May 29.

When the battle ended, American forces held only 28 prisoners; the rest of Yamasaki's soldiers were either dead or hiding in caves where, when discovered, all preserved their honor by committing suicide. The Battle of Attu was costly for Americans as well: 549 combat deaths, 1,148 wounded, plus other casualties due to illness and accidents—3,829 total casualties. Relative to the numbers who took part, it ranked among America's deadliest Pacific engagements, second only to Iwo Jima.

The battle for Kiska took a different course. Between June and early August 1943, U.S. aircraft dropped more than 1,000 tons of explosives on the tiny island, while warships shelled Japanese positions. American commanders did not know that under heavy fog at the end of July, Kiska's 5,000 defenders escaped aboard submarines and surface vessels. When 35,000 American and Canadian troops scrambled ashore on August 14, they found the island abandoned.

But victory obscured some unheroic undertones. Authorities imposed racial segregation on troops and Natives, and deported Japanese American citizens to internment camps. Following Japan's Dutch Harbor raid, over 800 Aleuts were abruptly relocated—as civilians in a combat zone—to deserted canneries in Alaska's Southeast. It was done for their protection, but conditions there were wretched and lacked medical services. Some died. When others returned home, many found their dwellings and churches vandalized by American forces.

The "Military Rush" and the Alaska Highway

G.I. work crew on the Alaska Highway near Whitehorse, Yukon Territory, 1943.

World War II proved to be the key event in promoting Alaska's modern development. By bringing defense dollars and tens of thousands of people northward—and highlighting Alaska's strategic importance—the war paved the way for statehood.

Germany's devastating air attack on Rotterdam in mid-May 1940, threw a scare into Congress, which immediately authorized construction of Fort Richardson, a large air base near Anchorage. From then on, troop movements into Alaska and congressional appropriations for military bases, air strips, and housing grew rapidly. A "military rush" was on.

The huge problems of supplying forces in the North Pacific contributed enormously to Alaska's long-term economic development. Coal mining expanded on the Kenai Peninsula, and oil pipelines were laid to reserves in Canada (Alaska's own reserves were yet undiscovered). Then on February 11, 1942, President Roosevelt authorized construction of the "Alaska Canada Military Highway," popularly dubbed the "Alcan."

Built in just eight and one-half months in 1942, the Alaska Highway spanned more than 1,400 crooked miles between Dawson Creek, British Columbia, and Delta Junction near Fairbanks. Crews directed by the U.S. Army Corps of Engineers began work on March 9, moving toward one another from opposite ends of the road. The highway linked a string of air strips, previously built for the purpose of moving leased aircraft to America's war-time ally, Soviet Russia. The effort gained new urgency after Japan's early-June attack on Dutch Harbor in the Aleutians.

Soldiers and civilian contractors hacked the gravel road through unsurveyed bush, rock, and mosquito-ridden muskeg. Wilderness guides like the Yukon's Johnnie Johns blazed trail for the bulldozer convoy. Heavy equipment foundered in muddy ruts and bogs, and much was left to rust. An estimated 11,500 GIs, including many segregated black troops serving under white officers, labored on the project in 12- to 16-hour days. 7,500 civilians also worked on the road for a prime wage of $1 an hour.

The construction crews met on November 20 at Soldiers' Summit, near Kluane Lake in the western Yukon. The highway, which cost $138 million to build, became the last leg of an overland route stretching south to Montana—the first direct land route to Alaska and the Yukon. As the ribbon was cut, the first truck moved out toward Fairbanks. The convoys carried supplies for U.S. forces in the Aleutians and lend-lease equipment for Soviet Russia. But the main burden of northern supply fell on cargo ships, and the highway never assumed quite the military role it was designed to play.

The road opened to the public in 1948, and travelers, some 80,000 a year by the early 1990s, quickly took over. The road has played a key role in binding the Far North to the rest of the nation—psychologically as much as physically. Driving today's highway, now paved but under constant repair due to weather damage, remains an adventure—even though most of the original heaves and twists have been straightened. The modern road snakes from British Columbia's grain fields and aspen groves through the Yukon's peaks and valleys to the black spruce taiga of interior Alaska.

THE POLITICS OF STATEHOOD

Juneau in 1886. Winter and Pond photo.

Though isolated visionaries dreamed of statehood from the moment the United States bought Alaska, the idea received no serious consideration in Congress for almost a century. Critics scoffed at the region's remoteness and argued that its tiny population could not generate enough taxes to finance any local government. Powerful commercial interests also consistently opposed statehood. The Seattle-based salmon canning industry especially feared that Alaskan home rule would mean increased regulation and higher taxes. The turning point in Alaska's road to statehood came with World War II, which produced an economic boom bigger than even the gold rush.

Suddenly, "Seward's folly" became the "guardian of the north," a vital link in America's chain of defense. The ensuing military rush pumped more than $1 billion in government money into the region and doubled its population. The trend intensified when tensions with America's erstwhile Soviet ally (56 miles across the Bering Sea) led to the Cold War. During the Korean conflict, the Defense Department poured $250 million a year into Alaska. By 1950, 26,000 service men and women were stationed in the region, and Alaska's larger towns grew enough to support a sizable professional class. The area was finally ripe for statehood.

Alaska's territorial governor, Ernest Gruening, became the high-profile champion of statehood in the post-war era. An accomplished author and speaker, Gruening spearheaded the campaign in books, articles, and lectures throughout Alaska and the Lower 48. Alaska's nonvoting delegate to the U.S. Congress, E. L. "Bob" Bartlett, played an even more important role. Self-effacing and reserved in contrast to the flamboyant, often self-important Gruening, Bartlett was adept as a behind-the-scenes lobbyist. In 1950, due largely to his efforts, a statehood bill passed for the first time in the House of Representatives.

A similar bill died in the Senate, however, partly because of fierce opposition from the salmon canners led by lobbyist Winton C. Arnold. Intent on protecting the canneries, Arnold cloaked his opposition in shrewd arguments that Alaska's small tax base could not support local government, and that Native land claims should be settled before statehood. To break the log jam, proponents devised an effective tactic.

In 1955, the territorial Legislature approved a constitutional convention in Fairbanks to draft a constitution for the region. Statehood's backers intended to show that Alaskans had sound ideas about administering and financing state government. Within three months, delegates produced a draft document that was a model of practicality. It was an important step in proving Alaska's political maturity to Congress and the nation. The House once again passed a statehood bill in early 1958 and sent it on to the Senate. By a vote of 64 to 20, the Senate gave its approval on June 30. Seven days later President Eisenhower added his signature. (Eisenhower's reluctance was overcome partly by the efforts of C. W. Snedden, the *Fairbanks Daily News-Miner* publisher, who convinced his friend, Interior Secretary Fred Seaton, to lobby the President on Alaska's behalf.) On January 3, 1959, Alaska joined the union as the 49th state, the first new state since Arizona in 1912, eight months ahead of the 50th, Hawaii.

Building the Alaska Railroad. Effects of thawing permafrost, 1919.

GEOGRAPHY, CLIMATE, AND NATURAL EXTREMES

NOT ONE LAND, BUT MANY

Ivan Petroff's 1882 map of Alaska's physical features.

As even casual visitors to the region can attest, the Russian designation bolshaia zeml'a—the "Great Land"—is no misnomer. In truth, Alaska is not one land, but many. The distances are so immense and the diversity of terrain and climate so extreme that Secretary of State Seward predicted in an 1869 speech in Sitka that the region might have to be admitted to the Union as several separate states. Today, some Alaska residents—far removed from the hub of state government in Juneau—might complain that his advice should have been heeded.

Geographers identify six distinct regions in the state: the Arctic, the Interior, Western Alaska, Southwestern Alaska, Southcentral Alaska, and the Southeast. The island-studded Southeast, home to such cities as Sitka, Ketchikan, and Juneau, enjoys a mild, maritime climate similar to that of Seattle and the Puget Sound. In this northern rain forest, temperatures range from 20 degrees in winter to 60 degrees in summer, and annual rainfall in some places reaches 200 inches. Ketchikan receives an average of 13½ feet of rain a year.

The tundra steppe of the Arctic represents the region's other extreme. Lying north of the Brooks Range, the vast area's soil never thaws below a few inches, and precipitation totals less than 10 inches yearly. Between the two extremes lies the semi-arid, broken forest of the Interior taiga, where the thermometer can dive to −60 degrees or more in winter and killing frosts occur as early as August. Yet summer temperatures in the Tanana Valley around Fairbanks may reach 90 degrees. "She's a beautiful country," a veteran bush pilot once observed, "but she can be cruel."

Climate and landscape have had profound effects on Alaska's peoples, cultures, and development. Natives learned to adjust to even nature's most severe rhythms. But the processes of modernization have sometimes been foiled by Alaska's extremes. Most commercial agriculture, for instance, has yet to succeed in the Far North. And a crash project in the late 1960s to quickly build a road to the North Slope oil fields—and promote trucking in the process—became a river of muck when ill-conceived construction methods melted the permafrost.

Some would be thankful; the Great Land retains so much of its pristine wildness and solitude precisely because of its climatic and geologic extremes.

Arc of Fire: Volcanoes of the Great Land

The Valley of 10,000 Smokes, about 1917.

On St. John's Day, 1796, awestruck officials of the Russian-American Company witnessed an event of earthshaking dimensions from the cliffs of the Aleutian island of Umnak. Twelve miles offshore in the Bering Sea, a fiery mass heaved into view, accompanied by thunderous tremors and "flames of such brilliancy that on our island... night was converted into day."

After three days, the fire and smoke cleared to reveal a volcanic cone. An island, christened Bogoslof by the astonished onlookers, had been born. Bogoslof volcano gained a sibling in 1883 when a second cone burst from the sea, joined to the original cone by a thin isthmus.

Alaska contains an estimated 60 to 70 active or potentially active volcanoes, 10 percent of the world's total. The great majority comprise a chain that swings westward from the Anchorage vicinity 1,500 miles out into the North Pacific. Over the past 200 years, most have exploded at least once as the land is constantly remade. Mount Pavlov in the Alaska Peninsula ranks as North America's most active volcano, with over 40 recorded eruptions.

Alaska's most devastating eruption came with the June 6, 1912, explosion of the Novarupta vent beneath Mount Katmai on the Alaska Peninsula. People in Juneau, 750 miles away, heard the blast, and sulfuric fumes reached south to Vancouver, British Columbia. Three more major eruptions soon followed.

At Kodiak, 100 miles to the southeast, a local captain reported that the blast put people in "abject terror." A foot of ash fell over the island, and only lightning flashes broke through two and one-half days of darkness. The Aleut fisherman Ivan Orloff, working on the west side of the peninsula, wrote to his wife: "We are awaiting death at any moment. A mountain has burst near here so that we are covered with ashes in some places 10 feet deep." Fortunately Orloff's fears were not realized; because of Novarupta's remote location, no one died from the eruption.

Three years passed, however, before anyone ventured into the Katmai area to observe the devastation first hand. Between 1915 and 1919, the botanist Robert Fiske Griggs, commissioned by the National Geographic Society, led four expeditions into the area. Griggs was overwhelmed by what he saw, particularly the vast basin of sulfur vents that looked like an ash-covered moonscape, which he named the "Valley of Ten Thousand Smokes." His reports to the society led President Wilson to declare the area a national monument in 1918. Today the smokes have all but disappeared and the former monument—the core of the now-enlarged Katmai National Park and Preserve—has become famous for its many brown bears.

Among the more restless summits in recent years have been Mounts Redoubt, Augustine, and Spurr on the west side of Cook Inlet, near Anchorage, where much of Alaska's population is concentrated. Between 1989 and 1990 Mount Redoubt erupted several times, sending ash over the Anchorage area and the Kenai Peninsula. In 1992 Mount Spurr took its turn, dumping a quarter-inch of ash over Anchorage and the nearby Matanuska-Susitna valleys. No wonder today's Alaskans regard the arc of fire with a mix of marvel and fear.

EARTHQUAKES AND TSUNAMIS

Earthquake damage in downtown Anchorage, 1964.

One in every 10 of the world's earthquakes occurs in Alaska, the result of nearly constant movement along segments of the earth's crust that geologists call tectonic plates. Fault lines related to these plates cleave Alaska's landscape and coastal sea floor, sometimes in dramatic fashion. The beautiful fjord known as the Lynn Canal, running from Skagway almost down to Juneau, is an example of just such a fault. Most of the state's quakes originate in the Aleutians, but all of southern Alaska is seismically active. Valdez, the southern terminus of the Alyeska oil pipeline, typically has one tremor a year of magnitude 5.0 or more on the Richter scale.

Violent earth tremors beneath the sea sometimes create a moving wall of water, known as a tsunami (Japanese for "sea wave"). Popularly misnamed "tidal waves" (they actually have nothing to do with tides), this kind of seismic ocean wave poses such danger to coastal towns that Alaska maintains a Tsunami Warning Center. Another type of wave linked to earthquakes is the seiche, or splash wave. The largest on record was produced by a tremor of magnitude 7.9 near Yakutat on July 9, 1958. The quake dumped 40 million cubic yards of earth into Lituya Bay, sending a wave 1,740 feet up the mountain on the opposite shore which then roared back down the slope and out to sea.

On Good Friday, March 27, 1964, at 5:36 P.M., southcentral Alaska rocked for three minutes from an earthquake centered in Prince William Sound. The quake registered 9.2 on the Richter scale—the mightiest quake ever registered in North America, and 80 times as powerful as the 1906 San Francisco earthquake. The earthquake caused tsunamis that did severe damage not only to Alaska communities, but to coastal towns as far away as Depoe Bay, Oregon, and Crescent City, California. In Alaska itself, the towns of Anchorage, Valdez, Seward, and Kodiak were hit the hardest. Tremors and a tsunami completely destroyed the original town site of Valdez; the new town stands on a more protected, geologically stable site four miles away. Many buildings in downtown Anchorage were either destroyed or heavily damaged. In all, 115 people were killed, surprisingly few in light of the size of the tremor. Fortunately, the earthquake hit in the late afternoon at the end of the work week, when schools and offices were closed and downtown areas were not crowded.

But property losses were enormous—an estimated $205 million. The new state, already hard pressed financially due to its small tax base, simply could not handle the situation. Alaskans willingly turned to "outside interests" for help. Fortunately, the federal government acted swiftly, providing millions of dollars in direct aid as well as social services assistance and low-interest loans. With such help, the state recovered in a remarkably short time. But the "Black Friday" quake left a vivid imprint on the memories of modern Alaskans, one reinforced whenever major new tremors occur—like the 7.1 and 7.0 quakes near Anchorage in 2016 and 2018.

MOUNTAINEERS AND DENALI

Conquerors of Denali: Walter Harper (white parka) and Hudson Stuck, 1917.

Alaska contains over 65 mountains above 10,000 feet in altitude. Greatest of all is 20,310 ft. Denali, which means "the High One" in Athabascan. Measurements in 2015 corrected the mountain's official height *downward* by 10 feet, from 20,320 to 20,310 feet. It is still not only Alaska's tallest peak but the highest in North America. The prospector W.A. Dickey originally named it Mount McKinley in 1896, after Ohio presidential candidate William McKinley. To honor Native traditions the state of Alaska changed the name to Denali in 1975, despite the protests of Ohio congressmen. President Obama finally approved federal recognition of the name change in 2015.

The mountain's early climbing history is as colorful as the story of Alaska itself. Natives generally stayed away from the peak out of reverence and fear, and so apparently never climbed it. Federal Judge James Wickersham was the first person to attempt the ascent, leading a party in 1903. But the judge turned back at 8,000 feet after encountering a face of ice, since known as the "Wickersham Wall." Wickersham declared that the mountain would never be scaled. Within 10 years he was proven wrong, but only after a string of intriguing scams and failures.

In 1906 Frederick Cook announced that he and a companion had conquered the mountain. Cook provided detailed reports of the alleged climb, as well as a photograph of himself on the summit, which was actually taken on a much lower peak. He was hailed by a gullible New York press, but experienced alpinists doubted Cook could have completed the expedition in the time he reported. Cook was a celebrity, nonetheless—evidently what he craved. While the controversy flared, he disappeared, announcing upon his return that he had reached the North Pole (only later was it discovered that this too was faked).

Cook's claims did not play well in the saloons of Fairbanks where, in late 1909, a group of miners led by Tom Lloyd decided no Easterner should be first to reach Denali's summit. Thus, arose the "Sourdough Expedition." Lloyd and six partners—none with climbing experience—set off in the dead of winter. Before they reached the mountain, a fistfight broke out, and three turned back. The remaining four began their assault in March 1910, without ropes and carrying a 14-foot flagpole to plant at the top. Luck was with them; the weather was good, and they had chosen, by chance, the easiest route. In a remarkable sustained climb of 18 hours, two of the party negotiated the final 9,000-foot ascent of Denali's north peak, planted their pole, and came down—unaware that the south peak was actually 850 feet higher. They had not reached the true summit, but their exploit is still considered one of mountaineering's most astonishing feats.

The mountain was finally mastered in 1913 by the missionary Hudson Stuck and three friends, including Stuck's Native sled driver, Walter Harper—the first man to set foot on Denali's summit. Since then, perhaps 32,000 climbers have challenged the peak and roughly 50 percent have succeeded. Technically, it is not one of the world's more difficult climbs, but the mountain's elevation and bitter weather demands proper respect from even veteran climbers. To date, it has claimed the lives of some 100 would-be conquerors.

Sydney Laurence and the Northern Landscape

"Mt. McKinley" by Sydney Laurence.

No artist is so closely identified with the Alaska landscape as Brooklyn-born Sydney Laurence, who lived between 1865 and 1940. Like every significant landscape painter, Laurence achieved two things: he seized something of the essential character of his subject, and he created enduring images that affect the way later viewers see that subject in their mind's eye. Even today his romantic renderings of trappers' caches, wild rivers, and—above all—unspoiled vistas of Denali's icy bulk define how Alaska's admirers envision the Last Frontier.

Like thousands of others, Laurence came to Alaska in search of gold. Before arriving in the Great Land, about 1904, Laurence studied painting and exhibited in New York, England, and France. He also had worked as an illustrator-correspondent in the South African Zulu War, the Spanish-American War, and the Boxer Rebellion in China. Though experienced and solidly trained before arriving in Alaska, he was not a noted or even commercially successful artist. At first, he produced few pictures, concentrating on a futile quest for gold. Later he explained matter-of-factly: "I was broke and couldn't get away. So, I resumed my painting." Establishing a painting and photography studio in Anchorage, he hit his stride as a full-time artist in the early 1920s. By the '30s he was making a comfortable living dividing his time between Alaska and southern California.

Laurence was an Alaska pioneer, but he was no pioneer of artistic method. As Kesler E. Woodward explains in *Sydney Laurence, Painter of the North*, he is largely known for his talent in employing "tonalist" ideas and methods shared by other American landscape painters of his day. He was also a skilled craftsman. No accomplished oil painter had previously tried to capture Alaska's landscape on such an extensive scale, and while some of his work is perhaps kitsch, his best pictures are consummate Alaskan portraits. Above all, he was able to establish an atmosphere through which viewers see the picture's subject. One tonally modified hue usually predominates—a pale rose, a golden yellow, a grayish green. By suspending that hue in a transparent, thinly layered series of oils or varnishes, Laurence created the impression that his vista was bathed in cloud or mist, conveying an authentic sense of seeing through northern light. In most of his pictures human figures are nonexistent or small and nondescript, dominated by an empty and untamed country. By subordinating people to an overpowering natural landscape, he established an enduring vision of the lonely, unspoiled wilderness frontier, one confirmed by the experience of many Alaskans or the imaginations of those who dreamed of Alaska.

Laurence's paintings, many produced on contract for sale in Juneau gift shops and Midwestern department stores, now command handsome prices—up to $500,000 or more—and dominate the walls of Alaska's museums and board rooms. In seeking to create their own visions of today's Alaska, new generations of artists struggle with the nostalgic conventions created by Laurence's work. And even today's most promising Alaskan artists find it difficult to escape the powerful theme of majestic country, overwhelming in its empty solitude.

New Deal Agriculture: The Matanuska Experiment

Matanuska colonists arriving at Palmer station, 1935.

Agriculture has always been Alaska's economic "Achilles heel." Russian colonizers failed to make the Great Land agriculturally self-sustaining—the daunting combination of northern latitudes, severe climate, and thin soils was overwhelming. To this day, American farmers have been scarcely more successful in claiming northern land for the plow.

The Matanuska Valley experiment of the Great Depression era is a classic illustration of the difficulties besetting Alaskan farming. In 1934, with considerable fanfare, the federal government invited people from poor rural areas of the northern Midwest to help found an agricultural colony in the picturesque valley between the Chugach and Talkeetna mountain ranges, 45 miles northeast of Anchorage. An agricultural station had been located there in 1915, and agronomists believed local soil and climatic conditions were suited to truck and dairy farming. The government promised land for as little as $5 an acre and offered free transportation from the Lower 48 and housing for the colonists. Ultimately, 202 families were chosen for the experiment. The town of Palmer became project headquarters, and officials promised a ready-made market for the immigrants' harvests: 9,000 people already lived in Anchorage and settlements extending northward along the Alaska Railway to Fairbanks.

The project appealed to public fantasies of the frontier and rugged individualism during the hard years of the Depression. However, little advance work was done before the colonists arrived in the valley in May 1935. No permanent housing existed, and only a survey of 40-acre tracts—drawn by lots on May 29—had been finished.

No sooner had the colonists arrived than Alaska's fickle climate greeted them with unseasonable rains throughout May and June. The newcomers lived in tents in an ocean of mud while helping government workers erect frame houses and other buildings. Meanwhile, their children succumbed to epidemics of measles and scarlet fever. Some families grew discouraged and gave up; embarrassed, the government paid their way back south and found replacements.

The colony survived but never flourished. Soil quality was uneven, colonists quarreled over the best land, bureaucratic regulation stifled initiative, and most settlers found 40 acres too little to make a go of things. In 1939 an early snow destroyed 80 percent of the grain and vegetable harvest. The creation of a military base at nearby Fort Richardson in 1940, on the eve of America's involvement in World War II, helped increase demand for Matanuska produce and, more importantly, provided part-time jobs for the farmers. Even so, the colony declined rapidly after the war's end.

In 1948 only 40 of the original pioneer families remained; in 1964 there were fewer than 400 farms in the entire state. Today some surviving valley farms provide welcome summer vegetables for local customers, but much of the old farmland has become residential suburbs for Anchorage commuters. While severe weather, poor soil, and the problems of long-distance marketing have so far stunted Alaskan agribusiness, the long summer days and lack of pests allow subsistence homesteaders and gardeners to grow a limited variety of hardy produce, sometimes of huge size—the giant cabbages of the Matanuska Valley being a famous example.

Sled Dogs and the Iditarod

Mail carrier leaving Circle City for Tanana, about 1900.

Nothing symbolizes Alaska so perfectly in the popular mind as a team of huskies drawing a pack sled across the frozen tundra. Until the advent of aviation in the 1920s, dogsleds, along with sternwheelers, were a vital means of travel, shipping, and communication in the Far North.

The dogsled originated at least 4,000 years ago in Siberia and was brought to Alaska by the nomadic ancestors of modern Indians and Eskimos. Native dogs, or malamutes, were hardly domesticated; to render them manageable their claws and incisors might be pulled, and males sometimes castrated. Even then the whip was required to prevent deadly fights. But without the stamina and uncanny sense of direction of these dogs, winter travel was scarcely conceivable; they even served as food in dire conditions.

In the Victorian Age, arctic explorers such as Sir Leopold McClintock and Fridtjof Nansen adopted the dogsled for their expeditions. During the gold rush, sled dogs proved indispensable for hauling provisions, equipment, and mail, inspiring Jack London's *Call of the Wild*. A famous gold rush trail was the Iditarod, which dates from 1910. Eventually stretching from Seward on the Gulf of Alaska to Nome (where gold had been discovered in 1898), the Iditarod—with roadhouses along the way—was a key overland route until the 1920s. In January 1925, mushing captured world headlines during a diphtheria epidemic in Nome. In blizzard conditions, life-saving antitoxin was delivered by dogsled relay in five and one-half days from the railhead in Nenana, 674 miles away.

Organized sled dog racing began in 1908 in Nome, which for several years hosted the All-Alaskan Sweepstakes and produced the sport's earliest celebrities: Scotty Allan and his mongrel lead dog Baldy, and Leonhard Seppala (later prominent in the 1925 serum run). The Siberian husky was introduced to Alaska by Seppala and became the premier racing dog. The Nome race died during World War I, however, and mushing rapidly declined with the advent of aviation. Sled dogs for winter transport persisted among Natives and others in the bush down to the 1960s but were then supplanted by the snowmobile. The last mail run by dogsled—to Savoonga on St. Lawrence Island—ended in 1963.

In 1966 Dorothy Page of Wasilla, president of a local committee organized to celebrate the centennial of Alaska's purchase, came up with the notion of the modern Iditarod race. She won the support of Joe Redington, Sr., a hunting guide and kennel operator who had an evangelist's passion for the dying art of mushing. As a result of their dedicated efforts, the first Iditarod Race, inspired by pioneer Nome's All-Alaska Sweepstakes, was successfully staged over a 25-mile course in February 1967, with 58 entrants and a combined purse of $25,000. Seppala had just died, and—in a touching gesture—his widow spread his ashes on the trail. But for several years thereafter interest declined, and it seemed the race might die.

Somehow Redington kept the idea alive and even proposed the course be extended all the way to Nome. Today the thousand-mile Iditarod, with a victor's purse of $50,000 or more, is an international sports event, and multiple winners like Rick Swenson and Susan Butcher are legends. Yet troubles have bedeviled recent races—dog-doping rumors, animal rights protests, sponsor withdrawals, warm weather—and some ponder its future.

Mining huts in the Silver Bow Basin near Juneau, late 1880s.

ECONOMICS AND
THE ENVIRONMENT

Growth, Conservation, Preservation: Alaska's Essential Tension

Hiker in Noatak National Preserve, Northwest Arctic. Karen Jettmar photo.

Alaska today—once a remote area, far past the frontier—has become one of the world's major laboratories for experiments in the three modern approaches to economics and the environment—growth, conservation, preservation.

Whether it's the battle over the harvest of salmon and crab, the hunting and regulation of the state's big game, or the discovery and exploitation of the Far North's huge oil reserves, advocates of these three approaches are locked in ongoing debate over what is best for the future of the Last Frontier.

From the minute the United States purchased the region from Russia, Alaska had its apostles of economic growth and population increase. Hard on the heels of the U.S. Army in 1867 came a group of nomadic entrepreneurs who envisioned Sitka as the next San Francisco. To such pioneers, frontiers existed to be eradicated. Manifest Destiny was in the air; "wilderness" was a term of disparagement. From the standpoint of most people there were wild lands and wildlife to spare, and not nearly enough civilization.

Still, by the 1870s the now-fashionable concept of "ecology" was beginning its modern career via the books of Darwinian biologist

Ernst Haeckel in far-off Germany. In time, the modern conservation movement began to take shape, aided by some obvious ecological disasters: the extinction of entire bird species and the slaughter of the great buffalo herds of the American plains. By the turn of the 20th century, the movement had attracted such vocal champions as big-game hunter and president, Theodore Roosevelt. The conservation movement got its start in the idea that wildlife should be protected and managed to ensure continued human use. This "resource husbandry" idea underpins much establishment thinking about economics and the environment today.

Despite conservationism, industrial development and rapid population growth continue to diminish the natural world. Wider, global forces give modernization a dynamism of its own. Through the planning or foresight of no one in particular, for instance, World War II—with its injections of people and money into the Far North—was in some ways a point of no return in the story of the Great Land.

The impact of such changes and the corresponding sense of loss gave rise to a new romanticism, a new nostalgia for the past, and a renewed spirit of stewardship. Since World War II, that third, "preservationist" attitude has blossomed. It overlaps to some degree with the utilitarian conservation movement, but its roots also reach farther back to romantic, early Victorian-era ideas of nature as a temple, not a workshop. Preservationism seeks to protect wilderness not merely for human use, but to cherish it for its own sake.

A hallmark of public consciousness in recent decades has been increased environmental awareness. The preservationist impulse is reflected in recent efforts to safeguard Alaska's natural resources and ecology—to protect Alaska's wild lands and nurture its natural heritage. And, one might add, its Native human heritage as well—the traditions of the aboriginal peoples, at once alien, timeless, and majestic, which seem so much to modern eyes like natural extensions of Alaska's physical landscape and space.

THE STORY OF SALMON

Small boy and king salmon, early 1920s.

Before the turn of the century, Alaskan waters teemed with five varieties of salmon: king (also called chinook or spring), sockeye (or red), silver (coho), pink (humpback) and chum (dog). A staple in the Native diet, salmon's predictable abundance sustained the leisure and high culture of the region's Natives, from the Yup'ik along the Bering Sea to the Tlingit and Haida Indians of southeastern Alaska.

Pacific salmon are born in fresh water, then migrate to sea, and after several years return upstream to their freshwater birthplace to spawn and die. People have long timed their fishing to occur during these spring and summer runs. For the species to survive, large numbers must reach the spawning grounds. Natives speared them or caught them in traps. Aboriginal fishing was ingenious and efficient, but Native populations were small, and many fish found their way past the nets.

The grasp of the fish canning industry, however, posed a serious threat to the species. The first Alaska canneries were built in 1878. By the 1920s, following a surge in demand associated with feeding troops in World War I, fishing supplanted mining as Alaska's major industry. The beneficiaries of this "salmon rush" were the canning companies, which had lobbying clout in Washington, D.C.

Cutthroat competition reigned in the fishery, and harvesting methods devastated the runs. Canneries were built at the mouths of rivers with big runs, and weirs were erected to block any fish from escaping. Ten canneries crowded the mouth of the Karluk River on

Kodiak Island, for example, and in 1890 these plants alone packed 200,000 cases—and paid no license fees or taxes.

Damming was outlawed in 1889, but Congress failed to appropriate enough money to effectively enforce it. A handful of inspectors was appointed, but the agents often relied on company boats for transportation to the canneries. As runs diminished, the packers admitted the folly of damming streams and substituted fish traps.

Traps were efficient and cost effective; while allowing some escapement, they caught millions of fish and could often be manned by one attendant. Such traps continued to be used in Alaska decades after their prohibition elsewhere; only after statehood in 1959 were they outlawed. Resident fishermen, who couldn't afford to compete with big "outside interests," despised the canners. When some locals began to rob and sabotage the traps at the end of World War I, the Navy sent gunboats north to police them.

Congress passed a few laws in the 1920s to protect the salmon runs, but policing remained thin and overfishing continued. After World War II, decades of overharvesting—combined with the arrival of Japanese and Soviet fishing vessels in North Pacific waters— threatened a resource that once seemed inexhaustible. The 1967 cannery pack was the lowest since the 1880s, and commercial prospects looked dismal.

Federal and state salmon management in the 1960s and 1970s dramatically altered the situation. In 1972 Alaska restricted commercial salmon fishing to 12,500 permit holders. In 1976, Congress adopted the Magnuson Act, which created a 200-mile off-shore zone under strict U.S. control. Today we see a striking turnaround in runs and catches. The 1973 harvest of 22 million fish, for instance, increased six-fold by 1984 to 132 million.

THE FISHING INDUSTRY

Pacific American Fisheries operations, Kodiak Island, 1964.

Since Alaska's first canneries were founded in the 1870s, salmon has been king in the North Pacific fishery. The commercial value of Alaska's salmon catch in the 1980s roughly equaled that of all other species combined. Yet bottomfish, crab, and many other species thrive in the Bering Sea and Gulf of Alaska, where shallow banks and the confluence of arctic and warm Japanese currents combine to create one of the world's prime fishing grounds.

The 1988 value of Alaskan fish landings was more than four times that of the nation's second-ranked producer, Louisiana. In the same year, six of the nation's ten most productive fishing ports were located in the Great Land, with Kodiak leading all.

Early entrepreneurs recognized the potential of the Alaskan fishery and, with the salmon boom of World War I, commercial fishing became Alaska's premier industry. Herring abounded in North Pacific waters, but early efforts to develop an Alaskan herring fishery—unlike salmon—met with limited success. Between the 1890s and 1920s, Ketchikan and Juneau salteries shipped barreled herring to eastern cities, gutted and packed by workers imported from Seattle and Vancouver. In the end, Alaska could not compete with established herring producers in Scotland and Norway.

More successful was the early halibut fishery—so successful that within decades the stock was almost destroyed. Halibut thrive in deep, cold water, and may exceed 500 pounds. As an eating fish, halibut is second only to salmon—indeed, many prefer its more delicate taste—and with the advent of new icing techniques halibut was readily supplied to eastern tables. In a reversal of the relentless north-to-south extermination of the sea otter, the American and Canadian halibut fleets progressively depleted halibut grounds from Cape Flattery on Washington's outer coast to the Alaskan banks by the eve of World War I. Then, in an eleventh-hour display of self-restraint, American and Canadian authorities acted to save the species. A halibut conservation treaty of 1923 and subsequent conventions imposed restrictions that slowly revived the fishery. Today, with strict quotas, halibut is once more a major commercial species.

Beyond the perennial threat of domestic overfishing, a new and critical danger arose after World War II: Japanese and Soviet trawlers entered the North Pacific, working right up to the three-mile limit. The intruders were so numerous and so efficient that they jeopardized the entire fishery. In 1976, Congress adopted the landmark Magnuson Act establishing a 200 nautical-mile zone off all America's coasts. Foreign vessels may still operate within the 200-mile zone, but only under American controls. The Magnuson Act was a boon to Alaskan fishing, which reported record harvests in ensuing years. An exception was the entire Alaska king crab fishery, which declined badly in the 1980s due to domestic overfishing.

The fishing industry's fortunes are always uncertain, but many experts believe its future lies in marketing designed to increase Americans' fresh fish consumption, and in harvesting the Bering Sea's enormous pollock stocks for use in fish products such as surimi, an increasingly popular imitation crab developed by the Japanese.

Hunting in Alaska

Trophy hunter Dall de Weese in 1897.

The word "Alaska" evokes the image of big game: black, brown, and polar bear, moose, caribou, mountain goat, and sheep. As a virtual North American subcontinent, the region's vastness afforded free range for a profusion of herds and species. The human population was sparse—in 1890 roughly 32,000 people, perhaps 4,300 of them white—lived in an area nearly half the size of India. Hunting was synonymous with Native culture, but Native belief in the blood kinship of human and animal life encouraged conservation in some ways. More important was simply the low ratio of hunters to hunted, since Native practices—despite traditional beliefs—were on occasion as wasteful as those of wanton whites.

On one trip to Glacier Bay, for example, the naturalist John Muir grew livid when a Native companion, asked to bag a mountain goat for supper, boasted that he had killed 11 deer instead and had brought back only the fattest one.

With a few unhappy exceptions—the near extinction of the sea otter, the extinction of Steller's sea cow and the Alaskan musk ox, and the slaughter of walrus for ivory—the balance was not upset even in Russian colonial and early American days, again because people were few and far between. Hunting was mainly a matter of subsistence rather than sport, even during the gold rush. A few game laws were enacted after 1902, but the statutes, tailored to a pioneer setting, were weakly enforced by a small cadre of wardens. Residents required no hunting license at all before 1936; thereafter a resident big-game permit cost $1.

World War II altered the situation dramatically with its overnight influx of military personnel—transients adept with firearms and eager for trophies. In 1940 Frank Dufresne, head of the Alaska Game Commission, warned that "Alaska's game herds simply will not bear up under the hunting of several thousand additional hunters."

Unfortunately for Dufresne, the trophy seekers included Major General Simon Bolivar Buckner, Jr., Army commander in Alaska. Dufresne and his aide Jack O'Connor stood firm in refusing resident rights to military personnel, insisting they buy nonresident permits for $50—twice a private's monthly pay. Buckner sued the Game Commission for the right to hunt as a resident.

Amid the patriotism of the war, the courts and the Congress ruled in the Army's behalf. At the end of the war Dufresne's fears about soldiers having easy access to game were realized. Troops desperate to bag their trophy before heading home engaged in a last-minute slaughter.

After the Buckner affair the old-time hunting life was largely a thing of the past. The Cold War military build-up, statehood in 1959, and the oil boom of the 1970s meant heavy new population pressures. Today, managed trophy hunting is an important ingredient in Alaska's tourist economy. Controlled subsistence hunting is still allowed for rural people—especially Natives—but overall modern Alaska has had to adopt a regulatory strategy of bureaucratic enforcement, biological studies, and new parks and preserves to sustain its ancient yet fragile big-game legacy.

ALASKA'S MARINE HIGHWAY

The Malaspina *of the Alaska Ferry fleet, 1989.*

Following statehood in 1959, officials recognized the need for a seagoing ferry system in a region where many cities—including Juneau, the state capital—are inaccessible by road. The state's Department of Transportation created the "Marine Highway System" in 1963 to serve the ports of southeastern and southwestern Alaska. The original ferry fleet consisted of four vessels. With the state's later economic and population growth, today's fleet has expanded to eleven ships serving 33 ports spanning 3,500 miles—farther than a drive from Seattle to Key West.

In southeastern Alaska, ships serve Ketchikan, Wrangell, Juneau, Haines, Skagway, and 10 other smaller communities. These towns, in turn, are linked to Canada and the Lower 48 via Inside Passage service to Prince Rupert, British Columbia, and Bellingham, Washington. Since late 1989, Bellingham has served as the Marine Highway's southern terminus; in prior years it was Seattle. In southcentral and southwestern Alaska, the fleet serves 18 ports, including Cordova, Valdez, Seward, Homer, Kodiak, and Unalaska/ Dutch Harbor in the Aleutians.

The ferries, distinctively painted in the blue and gold colors of Alaska's flag, provide indispensable public transport for Alaskans year-round, and during summers contribute to Alaska's tourist trade by bringing thousands of visitors to the Great Land. Traffic on the system has increased dramatically since its inception, from 84,000 passengers and 16,000 vehicles in 1964 to present-day numbers of 320,000 passengers and 97,000 vehicles. A large proportion of the travelers are tourists in summertime, when ferries ply the waters each week between Bellingham and Skagway.

Most travelers are Alaskan residents, however, for whom ferries are a vital lifeline between ports. Yet the fleet's future is presently clouded by funding problems arising from declining state oil revenues. In 2019, Governor Mike Dunleavy ordered a review of the system's viability.

Each summer since the 1970s, luxury tour ships also have cruised Alaskan waters, giving a mighty boost to tourism—third only to oil and commercial fishing in the state's economy by the 1980s. It's the second chapter of Alaska's cruise-ship history; the more modest, pioneer phase—ignited by John Muir's Victorian paeans to Glacier Bay—was interrupted by World War II. By the early 1990s, over 20 ships sailed annually to Alaskan ports, carrying 300,000 passengers—40 percent of the state's visitors. The boom stalled in the 2008–09 economic recession, followed by a robust rebound. In 2014, Alaska cruise passenger visits beat visits to Las Vegas as the nation's top domestic vacation. By 2017, 33 ships sailed mainly from Seattle or Vancouver, Canada, carrying 1,089,700 of Alaska's nearly 2 million out-of-state visitors—57 percent of the state's tourist market and far more than its estimated 2018 resident population of 738,000. The market ranges from mega-sized 4,000- to 5,000-passenger ships on one end to small-ship ecotourism on the other. Analysts expect continued growth, with cruise lines launching such huge ships that Vancouver must contemplate building a new terminal to compete with Seattle.

THE OIL BOOM

The Trans-Alaska Pipeline 15 miles south of Livengood, Alaska, late 1970s.

Petroleum—"black gold"—carried Alaska to giddy, new economic heights in the 1970s. The big strike came in 1968 at Prudhoe Bay on the Arctic Coast of the Beaufort Sea, where Atlantic Richfield geologists discovered a field with a capacity approaching 10 billion barrels—the country's greatest oil bonanza. In 1969 the state held an oil lease auction, with drilling rights going to the highest bidders. From this sale alone the state earned over $900 million.

The task now was to move the arctic wealth to southern markets. The best solution, corporate leaders decided, was an overland pipeline. Under the name Alyeska Pipeline Company, a consortium was founded to complete the project. The costliest private undertaking in U.S. history, the Alyeska project involved building an 800-mile pipeline from Prudhoe Bay to the ice-free port of Valdez on Prince William Sound. The engineering problems were formidable: the line had to climb two mountain ranges and cross 350 rivers and streams.

The companies were eager to begin in 1969. But environmental concerns and Native land claims delayed the project for five years. A turning point came in 1972, when Arab oil producers halted deliveries to the United States to undermine American support for Israel. In the resulting oil crisis, the public saw an urgent need for Alaskan oil and Congress approved the project. Construction began in 1974.

The consequence was an oil boom—on an Alaskan scale. Like the stampeders of the 1890s, workers streamed into Fairbanks, project headquarters, where they earned an average of $1,200 a week. Waste and escalating prices meant that the estimated construction cost—$900 million—ballooned to $7.7 billion by late 1976. The first drop of Prudhoe crude finally flowed south on June 20, 1977. The initial flow was 300,000 barrels per day. Later, at peak capacity, the daily rate rose to 2 million barrels. Ironically, the flow of oil produced unexpected problems in the fuel market.

By the time the pipeline was complete, the oil crisis was over, world petroleum prices had fallen, and the influx of Alaskan oil created surpluses on America's West Coast. The predicted wellhead price had been $7.50 per barrel, but the actual price in April 1978 was $4.39. Even so, the state collected substantial oil royalties.

The high point of affluence came in 1981 when oil revenues generated royalties worth more than $10,000 for every state resident. Naturally, the boom fueled a huge increase in state spending. It also made possible the 1976 creation of a state-managed, public trust fund, The Alaska Permanent Fund, now the nation's largest trust. In 1983, the fund began paying an annual dividend of almost $1,000 to each Alaska resident six months of age and older.

By the 1990s the nation's thirst for oil made the question of opening the North Slope to further exploration a controversial issue, one complicated by environmental concerns over caribou habitat and public reaction to the *Exxon Valdez* tanker spill of 1989.

The 800-mile route of the oil pipeline.

THE SPILL

The name "Bligh" is burdened by sinister overtones in fiction and film, although the historical William Bligh was perhaps not quite the ogre portrayed in *Mutiny on the Bounty*. It gained a new aura of menace at 12:04 A.M. on March 24, 1989, when the *Exxon Valdez* oil tanker ran aground on Bligh Reef, named for him as Captain Cook's navigator in 1778. The Good Friday collision, the fruit of numerous causes (including Captain Joseph Hazelwood's negligence and his wheelhouse crew's fatigue and inexperience), ripped a slash that emptied 11 million gallons of oil into Prince William Sound. Two days later a storm began spreading the slick down 1,300 miles of shoreline, along the Kenai Peninsula and as far as Kodiak and the Alaska Peninsula. Seals, sea otters, whales, hundreds of thousands of birds, and untold numbers of salmon and herring perished, fracturing the region's ecosystem and jeopardizing the livelihoods of Native and non-Native fishers. At the time it was America's most devastating oil spill; today it ranks second worst, after Louisiana's Deepwater Horizon spill of 2010.

Big oil's environmentalist critics had warned of some such calamity. Alaskan environmentalism arose in the early 1960s, when a coalition of Eskimo villages, scientists, and lobbies like the Sierra Club and Wilderness Society defeated "Project Chariot," an Atomic Energy Commission plan to use nuclear blasts to create a harbor at northwest Alaska's Cape Thompson. Championed by physicist Edward Teller, the scheme presumed the Arctic was "empty space," a tabula rasa to test atomic power. Environmentalism's victory against Teller's hubris helped anchor ecology's now popular assumptions regarding nature's fragile, interlocking web in America's social mind, and the need for environmental impact studies. Preservationists scored a second success in the mid-'60s when they defeated an Army Corps of Engineers plan to build a Yukon River dam at Rampart Canyon. It would have flooded 5,000 square miles, creating a reservoir bigger than Connecticut. Boosters welcomed the project as an Alaskan TVA to entice the aluminum industry; it was killed by predictions it would displace 1,200 Native villagers and drown the breeding marshes of millions of migratory birds.

When oil's Prudhoe Bay bonanza was discovered in 1968, the

industry made hasty plans to build a pipeline from the Beaufort Sea to southcentral Alaska's port of Valdez. The pipeline's initial designs echoed projects in Texas and didn't account for such northern conditions as permafrost. Environmentalists, building on precedents established in the Chariot and Rampart struggles, blocked construction on these terms, and hotly contested hearings and impact studies delayed building the pipeline and Valdez oil terminal until the mid-1970s. A major worry was icebergs shed by the Columbia Glacier, which sometimes threatened shipping beyond the Valdez Narrows. It was to avoid such bergs that the *Exxon Valdez* deviated from the shipping channel on its night to remember.

The tanker's crew was responsible for the wreck, yet blame for the spill's long-term impact was broadly shared. Exxon had delayed introducing double-hulled ships, which would have limited the spill's size. Coast Guard oversight of shipping lanes was lax, and it was slow to respond. The Alyeska Pipeline Company didn't have sufficient legally required containment equipment on hand and the state was ignorant of the fact. It took several days for Exxon to assume responsibility and begin cleaning up. Over the next five years Exxon spent $2 billion scrubbing wildlife and beaches, but much subsurface contamination remained. Today it appears the environment has largely recovered.

Legal disputes continued for years. Exxon settled a civil case for harm to wildlife and public lands for $900 million in 1991. It also paid the state and federal governments $100 million for the criminal discharge of oil. A class action suit for punitive damages was filed on behalf of 34,000 plaintiffs harmed by the spill; in 1994 a jury found Exxon guilty and fined it $5 billion. But the company appealed, eventually to the Supreme Court. Many parties subsequently settled out of court. In a 2008 ruling, the Supreme Court reduced Exxon's liability to $500 million, leaving the remaining plaintiffs about $15,000 apiece. Despite all the damage, the spill couldn't diminish industry's quest for more oil, nor the state's thirst for oil taxes that provided most of its revenue.

Coming to Terms with Native Land Claims

Native mission school students, Sitka, about 1887.

In the years following the American purchase, Alaska's Native peoples lost many of their hunting, trapping, and fishing grounds. Because the hunting and gathering life required vast expanses, the basis for ancestral customs eroded. More generally, modern development created other problems: new diseases, racial discrimination, and alcoholism. From 1867 onward the government pledged to protect Native rights. But such promises were often largely a dead letter well into the 20th century. Not until 1924 were all American Natives granted citizenship in Alaska and nationwide.

At the turn of the century, assimilation into white culture was the favored solution to the problem of Native rights, and Natives were urged to use the Homestead Act for any land claims. In 1915 Judge James Wickersham, representing the most enlightened thinking of the day, told a gathering of Athabascan chiefs that if Natives refused to use the Homestead Act, white people would. And then, the Judge warned, "when all the good land is gone... the Indians are going to have to move over." One of Wickersham's Athabascan listeners put the Natives' response in a nutshell: "We want to be left alone... God made Alaska for the Indian people, and all we hope is to be able to live here all the time." Gradually, however, some Native leaders learned to use the courts. In 1912 the Alaska Native Brotherhood (ANB) was founded in Juneau by Tlingit and Tsimshian leaders, followed by the Native Sisterhood (ANS). From their "self-help" milieu arose William Paul, Alaska's first Native attorney and its first Native legislator in 1924. In 1945, Alaska enacted an anti-segregation law, backed by the ANB/ANS and Governor Ernest Gruening. After statehood in 1959 the land-claims movement intensified and, as its spearhead, the Alaska Federation of Natives (AFN), created in 1965, became the first alliance of all Native groups.

The Prudhoe Bay oil strike of 1968 brought the land claims issue to a head. Some Natives claimed lands over which the oil pipeline would run; the Alyeska project could simply not go forward without a settlement. In the feverish atmosphere of an impending oil boom, the matter was resolved on what seemed generous terms for Natives. On December 18, 1971, President Nixon signed the Alaska Native Claims Settlement Act (ANCSA). According to the law, Natives received title to 44 million acres—over 10 percent of the state. The landmark act also awarded Natives $962.5 million in compensation. All U.S. citizens of at least one-quarter Alaska Native ancestry born before December 18, 1971, were eligible for the benefits. The act was crafted to divide the riches among the various Native groups as fairly as possible, with safeguards to protect recipients. Thus, Native lands were declared tax exempt for 20 years. And eligible Natives did not receive property or money as individuals, but—depending on their place of residence—were awarded 100 shares of stock in one of 13 newly created regional Native corporations. These shares could not be sold for 20 years. The AFN originated the novel idea of stock companies.

Despite obvious short-term benefits for Alaska's first peoples, the act was controversial. Under its terms, shares in Native corporations became eligible for sale to non-Natives after 1991. Critics of the act wondered whether Natives might then lose their wealth because of debts, corporate failures and takeovers, or simply an inability to pay state taxes. To meet such concerns, Congress amended the original act in 1988 to provide permanent tax exemptions for undeveloped Native lands, and to require a majority vote by Native shareholders to sell any corporation shares. Even so, since ANCSA was hastily written to expedite the pipeline, it required many more revisions. Whether it offers a long-term foundation for Native rights and security remains debatable, but it's clear that it thrust Natives to the center of Alaska's politics and economy.

PRIDE AND PREJUDICE

Portrait of Elizabeth Peratrovich.

Racial prejudice was pervasive in America in the late 19th and early 20th centuries, and Alaska—despite its reputation as an egalitarian "last frontier"—was no exception. Paradoxically it was the region's original people, its Natives, who mainly suffered. Russian rule before Alaska's American purchase in 1867 had in some ways been less discriminatory. Imperial Russia was an iron-fisted autocracy, to be sure, whose socioeconomic bedrock before 1861 was serf bondage. Yet in Alaska—for pragmatic reasons—the Russian-American Company encouraged Russian-Native intermarriage. Its mixed-ancestry "creole" population became the backbone of RAC operations, enjoying tax exemption and other advantages. Under American rule, creoles became an underclass of "half-breeds," suffering the same bias and legal handicaps as "full-blooded" Natives. A form of citizenship was theoretically open to Natives, but only if they renounced affiliation with their traditional ways.

Natives throughout America, including Alaska, received full citizenship with voting rights in 1924, yet discrimination was still widely taken for granted. Neighborhoods and schools were segregated, and businesses often displayed "whites only" signs. The Alaska Native Brotherhood (ANB), founded in 1912, and its companion Native Sisterhood (ANS) worked to change things, and made some headway in the courts. But it was World War II that enabled a legislative breakthrough; it was tough to defend discrimination at home while opposing Hitler's racism—especially when Native men participated in the fight. The 1939 appointment of territorial governor Ernest Gruening, a fiery civil rights advocate, also changed things. Key players in the coming events were Elizabeth and Roy Peratrovich, a Tlingit couple who led the ANB and ANS. In 1941, shortly after Japan's attack on Pearl Harbor thrust America into the war, the Peratroviches wrote to Gruening denouncing the display of "No Natives" signs by some businesses around Juneau. "... all freedom loving people in our country were horrified," they declared, at the "No Jews Allowed" signs in Nazi Germany, yet a related bigotry existed in Alaska. They had earlier been humiliated when they unsuccessfully tried to rent in a nice Juneau neighborhood. Gruening respected their complaint, throwing his energy behind a campaign for an equal rights law in the legislature.

The first legislative debate on an anti-discrimination bill came in 1943. It failed due to a tie vote. Gruening urged the ANB to bolster support for a second try by endorsing Native candidates in the next elections. Two were elected. Meanwhile, opinion was inflamed by the case of Alberta Schenck, an Eskimo Irish teenager actually jailed for one night for not vacating a seat in the "whites-only" section of Nome's movie theatre. The bill's second legislative debate in February 1945 yielded a memorable confrontation. After a series of back-and-forth arguments, Juneau's Senator Allen Shattuck asserted: "Far from being brought closer together... the races should be kept further apart. Who are these people, barely out of savagery, who want to associate with us whites with five thousand years of recorded civilization behind us?" Following the debate, the chamber's rules allowed gallery observers to comment. Elizabeth Peratrovich, a poised and elegant woman, took the opportunity and declared: "I would not have expected that I, who am barely out of savagery, would have to remind gentlemen with 5,000 years of recorded civilization behind them of our Bill of Rights." During his attacks on the bill, Shattuck asked if it would eliminate discrimination. To this, Elizabeth replied: "Do your laws against larceny and murder prevent those crimes? No law will eliminate crimes, but at least you as legislators can assert to the world that you recognize the evil of the present situation and speak your intent to help us overcome discrimination." Her proud rebuttal was met by applause. Today it is widely credited with sealing the bill's victory. Mrs. Peratrovich died of cancer in 1958. In 1988, Governor Steve Cowper proclaimed February 16, the equal rights law's anniversary, as Elizabeth W. Peratrovich Day.

Caribou and North Country Politics

Caribou in the Arctic National Wildlife Refuge.

Arctic and subarctic Alaska and Canada are the last strongholds of the caribou, a genus of migratory deer that once roamed—buffalo-style—over northern North America. Barren-ground caribou winter in Interior forests and, with the coming of spring and its mosquito hordes, migrate hundreds of miles to calving grounds on the Arctic shore. The herds move constantly, depleting tundra grasses, flowers, mosses, and lichens along their path. To Natives, the caribou had always meant food, robes, and bone for tools and weapons.

Caribou and public policy have often intertwined in Alaska's recent history. In the 1920s, biologists reckoned caribou numbers were close to a million, yet population levels plunged in the 1930s, falling to 160,000 by 1950. According to one theory, timber wolves devoured inordinate numbers of fawns—a controversial notion that justified wolf bounties on the one hand and, conversely, helped inspire Farley Mowat's celebrated defense of wolves, *Never Cry Wolf*.

Alaska's territorial government spent $500,000 in wolf and coyote bounties between 1915 and 1950, but the main reason for the mysterious decline seems to have been a combination of caribou fertility, overgrazing, and human interference.

By the 1930s, the herds grew so large that they outstripped their food supply. Missionary Sheldon Jackson's well-intended effort in the 1890s to augment the Eskimo diet by introducing reindeer—domesticated caribou—from Siberia to western Alaska further complicated the situation. Jackson's reindeer proliferated and bred with wild caribou, increasing animal populations and producing strains less suited to the tough conditions of the wilderness—a classic case of the unforeseen consequences of ecological meddling. Though much less numerous today, caribou are on the increase and constitute Alaska's most abundant big-game species. They now number around 218,000 on northeast Alaska's Arctic coast.

In the 1980s, politics and the fate of caribou converged once more, as oil interests and environmentalists became embroiled over the future of calving grounds in the 19-million-acre Arctic National Wildlife Refuge. With the discovery of the Prudhoe Bay oil fields in the late 1960s, petroleum became the leading factor in Alaska's economy.

As immense as the Prudhoe fields were, the oil companies were eager to discover new fields to keep the Trans-Alaska pipeline flowing with North Slope crude. State agencies also coveted added tax revenues and royalties. In 1985 Chevron Oil drilled an exploratory well on property located within the federal refuge but on lands whose mineral rights belong to the Arctic Slope Regional Corporation, an Eskimo Native corporation. Though drilling results remained confidential, they sparked an intense oil lobbying effort—supported by the state and the Iñupiat Eskimo corporation—to open the refuge to further exploration.

Environmentalists and Gwich'in Athabascan Natives fought the proposal, citing the threat to calving rhythms of the Porcupine River caribou herd, which the Gwich'in people depend on. Legislation to open the refuge seemed on its way to approval in 1989, but the *Exxon Valdez* tanker spill turned public opinion against the measure. Efforts since to get the issue moving in Congress have failed despite the Alaska congressional delegation's whole-hearted support. The issue remains unresolved, though in 2019 President Trump seemed poised to open parts of ANWR to drilling. One thing seems certain: the conflict over the Arctic refuge will not be the last in which wildlife become caught in the political crossfire over Alaska's future.

Glacier Bay National Park and Preserve from a cruise ship.

PRESERVING
THE GREAT LAND

Renewed Traditions:
The Renaissance of Native Arts

Tlingit carver Nathan Jackson roughing out a totem pole, 1978.

Over the ages before European contact, Alaska's first peoples evolved rich ceremonial and craft traditions. Early explorers marveled at their skillful execution. But to other newcomers, ritual masks, cedar columns, and potlatch feasts were something to be eradicated by persuasion or prohibition. Today the North's Native peoples are rediscovering their cultural traditions. Shishmaref on the Bering Strait, for example, is a center of Iñupiat ivory and whale-bone carvers, and Interior Athabascans stage frequent celebrations of their heritage.

The revival among Tlingit, Haida, and Tsimshian Natives of Southeast Alaska is a case in point. Their totem poles, with their interlocking animal and human figures, were often misunderstood by early whites as graven images. In truth, these poles served varied and complex purposes. Most featured stylized crests such as Raven, Eagle, or Bear—emblems linked to traditions that explained the community's place in the cosmic scheme. Many were monuments to family lineage and honor, somewhat like the heraldic crests of European nobles. They featured symbols associated with a great family's ancestry. Others were "history" poles that proclaimed aspects of a clan's past; "legend" poles that portrayed legendary or actual events; "memorial" poles that celebrated a great individual; or even "shame" or "ridicule" poles meant to humiliate a rival. Native leaders commissioned these columns to mark important events, such as a potlatch or a chief's death. Few outsiders appreciated much of this. From the pulpit and the schoolmaster's desk, many white leaders—often with noble intent—sought to bring Natives into modern civilization.

Civilization exerted an equally magnetic pull on the Natives themselves. On his journey to Glacier Bay in 1879, John Muir noted that many were eager to hear the message of his companion, missionary S. Hall Young; the Alaska Native Brotherhood, founded in 1912 to promote Native rights, also urged adoption of white ways. By the early 1900s, many art traditions had vanished, while others survived only as items for the curio trade.

Yet the potlatch persisted, and scattered artisans kept tradition's thin thread alive. Ironically, the Great Depression helped preserve skills. In 1938 the U.S. Forest Service sponsored Native arts projects to create jobs at Totem Bight and Saxman Village near Ketchikan. Beginning in the 1950s and 60s the Native arts were increasingly informed by academic studies that helped restore the high quality of older work. Projects at the University of British Columbia and the B.C. Provincial Museum in Victoria produced careful analysis of the formalized conventions underlying Northwest Coast Native art, governing the distinct but intertwined aesthetic traditions of Alaska's Southeast, west coast Canada, and western Washington. At Seattle's Burke Museum, the studies of non-Native curator Bill Holm also promoted rediscovery of forgotten rules and renewed integrity of style. In Fairbanks, the University of Alaska was a major center for cultural research and arts education for all Native groups.

Growing interest in Native traditions has thus produced a renaissance of lost arts—from Alaska's Arctic to its Southeast—and with it a rebirth of cultural energy. A high-end gallery, corporate, and museum market now exists, extending to work by all Native groups. Figures like Ronald Senungetuk (Iñupiaq), Larry Beck (Yup'ik), Nathan Jackson (Tlingit), or David Boxley (Tsimshian) enjoy international reputations. The rebirth extends to heritage in general: traditional dancing, theatre, regalia, weaving, and indigenous languages. Social activism has fed the revival, since the preservation of tradition is a powerful means to strengthen self-respect, sense of community, and promotion of civil rights.

Last Frontier or Lasting Frontier?

Bear Glacier and Callisto Head, Kenai Fjords National Park.

Alaska as the "Last Frontier" is an idea familiar to all. "Frontier" is a magic word for Americans, no doubt due to its suggestion of freedom and the pioneering spirit. A frontier offers elbow room—unfettered breathing space to grow, explore, and prosper. But beyond this, the richly nostalgic, evocative term lacks firm meaning.

What kind of freedom, what kind of frontier? Does frontier imply a land of opportunity where rugged, self-reliant people wrest a living from the land? In some parts of Alaska—Anchorage, with its nearly 300,000 people, or parts of the Southeast—this sort of frontier is already a thing of the past. And beyond a certain point, rugged individualism is a double-edged notion. What sort of freedom, what kind of frontier can one realistically have in the modern world, with its exploding populations, voracious energy appetites, snowballing technical advances, and industrial pressures?

Part of the problem (and the solution, perhaps), lies in sheer numbers—the ratio of people to space. "Of what avail are forty freedoms," asked Aldo Leopold, "without a blank spot on the map?"

In some ways Alaska is fortunate in having been so remote for so long; there are still some blank spaces. The region's northerly setting caused it to miss out on the agricultural phase that domesticated more southerly frontiers. In that sense, Alaska's lack of agriculture was a blessing in disguise. And by the time modern economic and population pressures came to bear—especially after World War II—the conservationist and preservationist movements were gathering momentum.

In 1980, the public will to preserve some of the blank spots on Alaska's map inspired congressional passage of the milestone Alaska National Interest Lands and Conservation Act (ANILCA). In the more immediate sense, the law helped settle land claims by the state and Natives related to statehood in 1959 and the Alaska Native Claims Settlement Act of 1971—although its approval was bitterly contested by the state government, many Alaskans, and promoters of resource development. Prior to statehood, the federal government had owned and managed 99 percent of Alaska's land. Judge Wickersham and other reformers had championed early acts of conservation such as the creation of Mount McKinley National Park (1917) and Glacier Bay National Monument (1925). In this tradition, ANILCA established 10 new National Park Service units in Alaska and expanded previously existing McKinley (renamed Denali), Glacier Bay, and Katmai national parks. The act doubled the size of the U.S. national park system—a fact indicative of Alaska's vastness. National parks in Alaska now comprise over 10 percent of the region's area—39 million of the state's 365 million total acres. Moreover, many more millions of acres were set aside as wildlife refuges, national monuments, national forests, wilderness areas, and wild rivers—with a total of 131 million acres affected. By such acts, conservationist and preservationist groups seek to transform at least a substantial part of "the last frontier" into a "lasting frontier."

ANCSA and Its Discontents

The lot of Natives—and Alaska's historical trajectory—were so altered by the 1971 Alaska Native Claims Settlement Act that historian Stephen Haycox calls it modern Alaska's "most important development." The settlement of Native land claims permitted extraction of petroleum reserves that are the state economy's life blood. Via the corporations and wealth enabled by ANCSA, Natives gained clout in state—and even national—affairs. Today, leaders of the AFN (Alaska Federation of Natives) are among the state's powerbrokers. Organized, with over 15 percent of Alaska's population, Natives exert real public influence. Unquestionably, ANCSA was a blessing for Natives.

Yet the complex, hurriedly drafted, and often unclear law was a mixed blessing. It left a legacy of thorny problems and conflicts between "have" and "have-not" beneficiaries. A few Native corporations grew wealthy in global markets; most were marginally profitable, but some teetered on bankruptcy's tightrope. In the top tier, the North Slope Iñupiaq's lands held oil that generated fairy-tale wealth. The Cook Inlet Regional Corporation based in Anchorage made lucrative nationwide investments in technology and real estate. The Southeast's Sealaska Regional Corporation owned valuable timber reserves. Yet some groups had only subsistence homelands without rich minerals. Disagreements between the Iñupiaq and their Gwich'in Athabascan neighbors highlight conflicts of interest. The oil-rich Iñupiaq push to open the Arctic National Wildlife Refuge to petroleum development; the Gwich'in stoutly oppose it, fearing its impact on caribou migrations upon which their lives and folkways depend.

Modernization propelled by ANCSA spawns social disparity among Natives. At the top, an urban elite is adept at politics and corporate capitalism. In gold rush days, pioneer missionaries and politicians like Sheldon Jackson and James Wickersham preached the gospel of Native assimilation to white ways; willy-nilly, at the big-business level of ANCSA's 13 regional corporations, it has triumphed.

Yet things often differ in the rural villages, where most Natives live. Villagers widely suffer the ills of poverty, diabetes, domestic abuse, alcoholism, and suicide. There is special friction between subsistence villagers and the state. Many resent state regulations that they believe hamstring management of their resources. In accepting ANCSA, to be sure, they gained title to their homelands. Like property owners anywhere, however, they must abide by state and national laws. Under ANCSA, state and federal agencies regulate hunting and fishing, and the state even controls most health, education, and police matters. Many villagers think they could more prudently manage those affairs themselves, with their knowledge of local needs. Many believe their interests would be best protected by the self-governance, reservation model of the Lower 48 states, where tribal and federal authority often trump state law. Unlike the Lower 48, Alaska lacks reservations (except for the Tsimshian reserve of Metlakatla near Ketchikan). In pioneer Alaska, with its tiny non-Native population and lack of agricultural land, reservations were not created. Some New Deal reformers unsuccessfully promoted them in the 1930s; Natives themselves generally opposed them then, due to the stigmas of dependency and poverty linked to southern reserves. Today, though, after recent reforms to the southern model, reservations appeal to many Alaskan villagers. Court rulings in the 1990s seemed to suggest that tribal sovereignty on reservations is inconsistent with ANCSA, but another, "land trust" option is now on the table. Under this vision, villages could voluntarily place their land in trust to the federal government, which could then grant them increased control of fishing, hunting, and civil affairs. It would create self-governance akin to the partial sovereignty today's Lower 48 tribes enjoy. State officials generally oppose this tribal "land trust" idea because it would diminish the state's authority. Even some members of the Native elite are skeptical, fearing that increased federal oversight might complicate future development of mineral resources that might be discovered. In 2016 a federal appeals court ruled in favor of the "land-into-trust" idea, and the Obama administration accepted the judgment. In 2018 the Trump administration withdrew that policy, however, putting things into limbo once more. Alaska historian Claus-M. Naske's conclusion seems apt: "ANCSA is an experiment that is still evolving, and will be for a long time into the future."

The State of Alaska

Alaska's State Flag

The legacy of Alaska's Native land claims settlement is just one of many challenges facing the state. Their outcomes remain unclear. Receding glaciers, melting permafrost, and shrinking ice packs make the region a cockpit for debates on global climate change. For activists, the Eskimo village of Shishmaref—its shores eroding under seas unleashed by melting ice—is a "coal mine canary" for global warming. Warming oceans alter fish migrations and threaten fisheries. The frozen Northwest Passage is now sometimes navigable by cruise and even container ships. We're on uncertain ice when appraising today's shift, its probable length and pace, and the dire predictions of some pundits. Is this a relatively brief trend or the onset of an epic age of extreme climate change? Geology and recorded history show that climate cycles are normal. Alaska's Beringian prehistory underscores their impact on human evolution. In the short run, at least, a warming tendency seems to impact Alaska; it will likely produce problems, opportunities, and surprises.

Alaska's chief quandary is its reliance on oil. No other state depends so one-sidedly on a single depletable resource—one whose by-products are widely blamed for climate change. Windfall revenue from oil's discovery was manna that funded the fledgling state's financial needs. The state's population growth and the vibrance of its modern consumer culture hinge on oil's prices.

If oil was a blessing, one-sided reliance on it is not. Even if new oil is discovered, its value may drop due to global shifts to other energy sources. Alaska's economy is lopsided and linked to decisions made in distant corporate hubs, prompting some to claim it remains a "colony" of external powers. Stephen Haycox subtitled his sterling history of Alaska "An American Colony." Economist Donna Logan asserts that oil dependency makes Alaska look "like something you'd see in the Third World." Some Alaskans fume over federal controls, Native rights protections, and land-use restrictions they believe hamstring the state's freedom to grow. They contend Alaska was robbed of development lands by federal ANCSA and ANILCA land legislation.

Alaska was indeed a colony in Russian days and might be understood as colonial in U.S. territorial times. Imagining it as a colony today, though, can be overdone. The word "colony" is heavy with suggestions of exploitation and victimhood, echoing resentments of neglect and injustice stretching back to Judge Wickersham's muckraking crusades against "outside" interests. His attacks on manipulative Seattle canners and New York's Guggenheim financial barons were justified. Yet anger-and-resentment pathos today seems as unrealistic as "reality" television's tales of the rough-hewn "last frontier" life—which many modern Alaskans find phony. Alaska since 1959 enjoys state's rights and its situation is perhaps not so exceptional. Haycox affirms that federal policies have been constitutionally correct and usually prudent. And historian Claus-M. Naske may have a point: Alaska is indeed capital poor and dependent on world markets and decisions made in distant financial centers. But if this means colonialism, "virtually the entire planet is an economic colony of someplace else, especially in this era of globalization."

Like many regions, Alaska needs to diversify and generate its own capital, which is easier said than done. Tourism is a renewable resource but cannot fill a vacuum left by sagging oil revenues. Some observers suggest Alaskans may have to embrace slower growth and a smaller economic future, after their roller-coaster half-century of oil-boom. Since Russian times Alaska has depended on resource extraction and has weathered many boom-and-bust spikes of a world economy. Today's Alaska Permanent Fund was created because people knew oil's godsend wouldn't last forever. The Fund has been well managed—though in recent years its earnings have sometimes been tapped and dividends reduced to cover troubling state deficits.

We see the future, if at all, through a glass, darkly—but we can anticipate that it will surprise us. There is still oil in Alaska, and other minerals to be found. Some political change, discovery, or new technology may spark another big "rush" of the type that studs Alaska's past, but it's hard to imagine one on the scale of the Prudhoe Bay bonanza. Economist Adam Millsap draws a stoical conclusion: "Even a smaller Alaska can still be a great place to live and do business for the people who choose to call it home, and that is what Alaskans should focus on achieving." Alaska's stunning beauty will support tourism and attract residents who value the environment. Its strategic geopolitical location and today's environmentalist ethos will insure federal defense and ecological investments. And, while it is capital poor, it is the only state with a $60 billion "savings account" (the Permanent Fund, as of late 2018). This, Naske suggests, is reason to "question the claim that Alaska is just another downtrodden colony exploited by others."

RELATED READING

Berton, Pierre. *The Klondike Fever: The Life and Death of the Last Great Gold Rush*. New York: Alfred A. Knopf, 1958.

Billberg, Rudy. *In the Shadow of Eagles: From Barnstormer to Bush Pilot, a Flyer's Story*. Bothell, W.A.: Alaska Northwest Books, 1992.

Black, Lydia T. *Russians in Alaska, 1732-1867*. Fairbanks, A.K.: University of Alaska Press, 2004.

Black, Martha Louise. *Martha Black*. Ed. by Flo Whyard. Anchorage, A.K.: Alaska Northwest Publishing Company, 1976.

Boochever, Annie with Roy Peratrovich, Jr. *Fighter in Velvet Gloves: Alaska Civil Rights Hero Elizabeth Peratrovich*. Fairbanks, A.K.: University of Alaska Press, 2019.

Brown, Tricia. *Silent Storytellers of Totem Bight State Historical Park*. Anchorage, A.K.: Alaska Geographic Association, 2009.

Bruder, Jerry. *Heroes of the Horizon: Flying Adventures of Alaska's Legendary Bush Pilots*. Bothell, W.A.: Alaska Northwest Books, 1991.

Bruggmann, Maximilien, and Peter R. Gerber. *Indians of the Northwest Coast*. New York: Facts on File, 1989.

Chevigny, Hector. *Lord of Alaska*. New York: Viking, 1942.

Chevigny, Hector. *Russian America*. New York: Viking, 1965.

Cole, Terrence. *Fighting for the Forty-Ninth Star: C. W. Snedden and the Crusade for Alaska Statehood*. Fairbanks, A.K.: University of Alaska Foundation, 2010.

Crowell, Aron, Amy F. Steffian, and Gordon L. Pullar, eds. *Looking Both Ways: Heritage and Identity of the Alutiiq People*. Fairbanks, A.K.: University of Alaska Press, 2001.

Davidson, Art. *In the Wake of the Exxon Valdez: The Devastating Impact of The Alaska Oil Spill*. San Francisco, C.A.: Sierra Club Books, 1990.

Drucker, Philip. *Indians of the Northwest Coast*. Garden City, N.Y.: The Natural History Press, 1963.

Dyson, George. *Baidarka*. Edmonds, W.A.: Alaska Northwest Publishing Company, 1986.

Fitzhugh, William W. and Aron Crowell. *Crossroads of Continents: Cultures of Siberia and Alaska*. Washington, D.C.: Smithsonian Institution Press, 1988.

Fitzhugh, William W. and Susan A. Kaplan. *Inua: Spirit World of the Bering Sea Eskimo*. Washington, D.C.: Smithsonian Institution Press, 1982.

Ford, Corey. *Where the Sea Breaks Its Back: The Epic Story of Early Naturalist Georg Steller and the Russian Exploration of Alaska*. Bothell, W.A.: Alaska Northwest Books, 1992.

Garfield, Brian. *The Thousand-Mile War: World War II in Alaska and the Aleutians*. Garden City, N.Y.: Doubleday, 1969.

Gruening, Ernest. *Many Battles: The Autobiography of Ernest Gruening*. New York: Liveright, 1973.

Gruening, Ernest, ed. *An Alaskan Reader, 1867–1967*. New York: Meredith Press, 1966.

Haycox, Stephen. *Alaska: An American Colony*. Seattle, W.A.: University of Washington Press, 2002.

Haycox, Stephen. *Frigid Embrace: Politics, Economics and Environment in Alaska*. Corvallis, O.R.: Oregon State University Press, 2002.

Haycox, Stephen and Mary Childers Mangusso, eds. *An Alaska Anthology: Interpreting the Past*. Seattle, W.A.: University of Washington Press, 1996.

Hinckley, Ted C. *The Americanization of Alaska, 1867–1897*. Palo Alto, C.A.: Pacific Books, 1972.

Hirschmann, Fred (photography), and Kim Heacox (text). *Bush Pilots of Alaska*. Portland, O.R.: Graphic Arts Center Publishing Company, 1989.

Hunt, William R. *Alaska: A Bicentennial History*. New York: W. W. Norton, 1976.

Hunt, William R. *North of 53: The Wild Days of the Alaska-Yukon Mining Frontier, 1870–1914*. New York: Macmillan, 1974.

Luehrmann, Sonja. *Alutiiq Villages Under Russian and U.S. Rule*. Fairbanks, A.K.: University of Alaska Press, 2008.

Macnair, Peter L., Alan L. Hoover and Kevin Neary. *The Legacy: Tradition and Innovation in Northwest Coast Indian Art*. Vancouver, B.C.: Douglas and McIntyre, 1984.

Madden, Ryan. *Alaska*. Northhampton, M.A.: Interlink Press, 2005.

Miller, Gwenn A. *Kodiak Kreol: Communities of Empire in Early Russian America*. Ithaca, N.Y.: Cornell University Press, 2010.

Morgan, Murray. *One Man's Gold Rush: A Klondike Album*. Seattle, W.A.: University of Washington Press, 1967.

Muir, John. *Travels in Alaska*. Boston, M.A.: Houghton Mifflin, 1979.

Murie, Margaret E. *Two in the Far North*. Anchorage, A.K.: Alaska Northwest Publishing Company, 1978.

Naske, Claus-M. and Herman E. Slotnick. *Alaska: A History*. 3rd ed. Norman, O.K.: University of Oklahoma Press, 2011.

Potter, Jean. *The Flying North*. New York: Macmillan, 1947.

Sherwonit, Bill. *Iditarod: The Great Race to Nome*. Bothell, W.A.: Alaska Northwest Books, 1991.

Sherwonit, Bill. *To the Top of Denali: Climbing Adventures on North America's Highest Peak*. Anchorage, A.K.: Alaska Northwest Books, 1990.

Sherwood, Morgan B., ed. *Alaska and Its History*. Seattle, W.A.: University of Washington Press, 1967.

Sherwood, Morgan. *Big Game in Alaska: A History of Wildlife and People*. New Haven, C.T.: Yale University Press, 1981.

Sherwood, Morgan. *Exploration of Alaska*, 1865–1900. New Haven, C.T.: Yale University Press, 1965.

Smith, Barbara Sweetland, and Redmond J. Barnett. *Russian America: The Forgotten Frontier*. Tacoma, W.A.: Washington State Historical Society, 1990.

Stewart, Hilary. *Looking at Indian Art of the Northwest Coast*. Seattle, W.A.: University of Washington Press, 1979.

Vinkovetsky, Ilya. *Russian America: An Overseas Colony of a Continental Empire, 1804-1867*. New York: Oxford University Press, 2011.

Webb, Robert Lloyd. *On the Northwest: Commercial Whaling in the Pacific Northwest, 1790–1967*. Vancouver, B.C.: University of British Columbia Press, 1988.

Wickersham, James. *Old Yukon: Tales—Trails—and Trials*. Washington, D.C.: Washington Law Book Co., 1938.

Woodward, Kesler E. *Sydney Laurence, Painter of the North*. Seattle, W.A.: University of Washington Press, 1990.

Young, S. Hall. *Alaska Days with John Muir*. New York: Fleming H. Revell, 1915.

INDEX

Photo Credits

Page 2: Special Collections Division, University of Washington Libraries, Winter and Pond photo #NA-2663. 5: Alaska Historical Library, Case and Draper Collection, PCA 39-843. 8: Alaska Historical Library, Clyda Scott Greely Collection, PCA 66-368. 12: Center for Pacific Northwest Studies, Western Washington University. 14: Dept. of Special Collections, Stanford University Libraries, 917.8 A323. 16: Special Collections Division, University of Washington Libraries, Harriman Album, Curtis photo #NA 21016. 18: Special Collections Division, University of Washington Libraries, Harriman Album, Curtis photo #7791. 20: Center for Pacific Northwest Studies, Western Washington University. 21: Center for Pacific Northwest Studies, Western Washington University. 22: Special Collections Division, University of Washington Libraries, #13115. 24: National Anthropological Archives, SI-6362. 26: Special Collections Division, University of Washington Libraries, Harriman Album, Curtis photo #NA 2129. 30: Special Collections Division, University of Washington Libraries, Webster and Stevens photo #472a. 32: Dept. of Special Collections, Stanford University Libraries, 917.98 A323, No. 188. 34: Center for Pacific Northwest Studies, Western Washington University. 36: Special Collections Division, University of Washington Libraries, #13188. 38: Courtesy of Museum of New Mexico. 40: Archives, Alaska and Polar Regions Dept., University of Alaska Fairbanks, Historical Photograph Collection, acc. #68-12-56N. 42: Special Collections Division, University of Washington Libraries, LaRoche photo #1108. 44: Special Collections Division, University of Washington Libraries, Heath Collection, Winter and Pond photo #14506. 46: Special Collections Division, University of Washington Libraries, Cantwell photo #46. 48: Special Collections Division, University of Washington Libraries, #8165. 50: Archives, Alaska and Polar Regions Dept., University of Alaska Fairbanks, Historical Photograph Collection, acc.#72-164-IN VF. 52: Alaska State Library, Collection: A Summer on the Thetis, 1888, PCA 27-70. 54: Alaska Historical Library, Early Prints of Alaska #01-1222. 56: Dept. of History, Presbyterian Church (USA). 58: U.S. National Park Service. 60: Special Collections Division, University of Washington Libraries, Partridge photo #Na. 7791. 62: Archives, Alaska and Polar Regions Dept., University of Alaska Fairbanks, Charles E. Bunnell Collection, acc. #58-1026-1099. 64: Special Collections Division, University of Washington Libraries, Hegg photo #3779. 66: Center for Pacific Northwest Studies, Western Washington University. 68: Archives, Alaska and Polar Regions Dept., University of Alaska Fairbanks, W. F. Erskine Collection, acc. #78-28-715 and #70-28-802n. 70: Special Collections Division, University of Washington Libraries,

Partridge photo #7964. 72: Special Collections Division University of Washington Libraries, Partridge photo #14504. 74: U.S. National Archives. 76: Alaska Historical Library, Collection: Early Prints of Alaska, #01-3338. 78: Special Collections Division, University of Washington Libraries, Nowell photo #14507. 80: Special Collections Division, University of Washington Libraries #8069. 82: Alaska Historical Library, Clyda Scott Greely Collection, PCA 66-268. 84: Archives, Alaska and Polar Regions Dept., University of Alaska Fairbanks, acc. #67-44-3n and 81-24-102. 86: Archives, Alaska and Polar Regions Dept., University of Alaska Fairbanks, Frederick Machetanz Collection, acc. #73-75-1428. 88: Photo by Fred Goodman. 90: Special Collections Division, University of Washington Libraries, Winter and Pond photo #14502. 90: Archives, Alaska and Polar Regions Dept., University of Alaska Fairbanks, Frederick Mears Collection, acc. #84-75-354. 94: Wilson Library Special Collections, Western Washington University. 96: Archives, Alaska and Polar Regions Dept., University of Alaska Fairbanks, Kirtley Fletcher Mather Collection, acc. #82-178-109. 96: Special Collections Division, University of Washington Libraries, #14501. 98: Archives, Alaska and Polar Regions Dept., University of Alaska Fairbanks, Frederick Drane Album #2, acc. #91-046-531. 102: Archives, Alaska and Polar Regions Dept., University of Alaska Fairbanks, Lulu Fairbanks Collection, acc. #68-69-84. 104: Alaska Historical Library, Mary Nan Gamble Collection, PCA 270-224. 106: Whatcom Museum of History and Art, Moran Bros. Collection, No. 74. 108: Dept. of Special Collections, Stanford University Libraries, 917.98 A323, No. 202. 110: Photo by Karen Jettmar. 112: Whatcom Museum of History and Art, J.W. Sandison Collection, No. 710. 114: Center for Pacific Northwest Studies, Western Washington University. 116: Special Collections Division, University of Washington Libraries, #8248. 118: Port of Bellingham. 120: Special Collections Division, University of Washington Libraries, #14505. 121: Special Collections Division, University of Washington Libraries, #14503. 124: Special Collections Division, University of Washington Libraries, Partridge photo #NA 2552. 126: Alaska State Library–Historical Collections. 128: Photo by Ken Whitten. 130: Photo by the author. 132: Tongass Historical Museum, City of Ketchikan. 134: Photo by the author.

ABOUT THE AUTHOR

Harry Ritter is Emeritus Professor of History at Western Washington University, where he taught from 1969 to 2010. Born in St. Louis, Missouri, he received his doctorate in history from the University of Virginia. He is also the author of *Washington's History: The People, Land, and Events of the Far Northwest*. He lives in Bellingham, Washington.